PRESENTED TO:

Renee Roberts

GIVEN BY:

Blake Roberts & Sara Lindsey

A SPECIAL NOTE:

Birthday Gift
5-28-2014

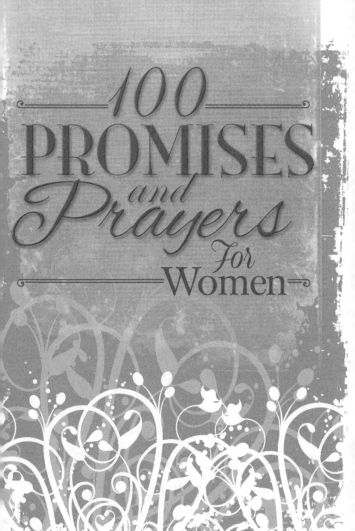

100
PROMISES
and
Prayers
For
Women

ISBN 978-1-60587-529-3

Published by Freeman-Smith, a division of Worthy Media, Inc.,
134 Franklin Road, Suite 200, Brentwood, Tennessee 37027.

The quoted ideas expressed in this book (but not Scripture verses) are not, in all cases, exact quotations, as some have been edited for clarity and brevity. In all cases, the author has attempted to maintain the speaker's original intent. In some cases, quoted material for this book was obtained from secondary sources, primarily print media. While every effort was made to ensure the accuracy of these sources, the accuracy cannot be guaranteed. For additions, deletions, corrections, or clarifications in future editions of this text, please write Freeman-Smith.

The Holy Bible, King James Version

The Holy Bible, New King James Version (NKJV) Copyright © 1982 by Thomas Nelson, Inc. Used by permission.

New century Version®. (NCV) Copyright © 1987, 1988, 1991 by Word Publishing, a division of Thomas Nelson, Inc. All rights reserved. Used by permission.

The Holman Christian Standard Bible™ (HCSB) Copyright © 1999, 2000, 2001 by Holman Bible Publishers. Used by permission.

The Holy Bible, New International Version®. (NIV) Copyright © 1973, 1978, 1984 International Bible Society. Used by permission of Zondervan. All rights reserved.

The Holy Bible. New Living Translation (NLT) copyright © 1996 Tyndale Charitable Trust. Used by permission of Tyndale House Publishers.

The New American Standard Bible®, (NASB) Copyright © 1960, 1962, 1963, 1968, 1971, 1972, 1973, 1975, 1977, 1995 by The Lockman Foundation. Used by permission.

Scripture taken from The Message. (MSG) Copyright © 1993, 1994, 1995, 1996, 2000, 2001, 2002. Used by permission of NavPress Publishing Group.

Cover Design by Kim Russell / Wahoo Designs
Page Layout by Bart Dawson

Printed in the United States of America

1 2 3 4 5—CHG—17 16 15 14 13

100
PROMISES
and
Prayers
For
Women

INTRODUCTION

How desperately our world needs Christian women who are willing to honor God with their prayers and their service. Hopefully, you are determined to become such a woman—a woman who walks in wisdom as she offers counsel and direction to her family, to her friends, and to her coworkers.

This generation faces problems that defy easy solutions, yet face them we must. We need women whose vision is clear and whose intentions are pure. And this book can help.

In your hands, you hold a book that contains 100 devotional readings. These readings contain Bible promises, prayers, brief essays, and inspirational quotations from noted Christians.

During the next 100 days, please try this experiment: read a chapter from this book each day. If you're already committed to a daily time of worship, this book will enrich that experience. If you are not, the simple act of giving God a few minutes each morning will change the direction and the quality of your life.

Each day provides opportunities to put God where He belongs: at the center of our lives. When we do so, we worship Him, not just with words, but with deeds. And, we become dutiful servants of God, righteous women who share His Son's message of love and salvation with the world.

May you be such a woman—and may you always be a woman of prayer.

DAY 1

LISTENING TO GOD

The one who is from God listens to God's words.
This is why you don't listen,
because you are not from God.
John 8:47 HCSB

Sometimes God speaks loudly and clearly. More often, He speaks in a quiet voice— and if you are wise, you will be listening carefully when He does. To do so, you must carve out quiet moments each day to study His Word and sense His direction.

Can you quiet yourself long enough to listen to your conscience? Are you attuned to the subtle guidance of your intuition? Are you willing to pray sincerely and then to wait quietly for God's response? Hopefully so. Usually God refrains from sending His messages on stone tablets or city billboards. More often, He communicates in subtler ways. If you sincerely desire to hear His voice, you must listen carefully, and you must do so in the silent corners of your quiet, willing heart.

The first service one owes to others in the fellowship consists in listening to them. Just as love of God begins in listening to His Word, so the beginning of love for the brethren is learning to listen to them.

Dietrich Bonhoeffer

The center of power is not to be found in summit meetings or in peace conferences. It is not in Peking or Washington or the United Nations, but rather where a child of God prays in the power of the Spirit for God's will to be done in her life, in her home, and in the world around her.

Ruth Bell Graham

TODAY'S PRAYER

Lord, give me the wisdom to be a good listener. Help me listen carefully to my family, to my friends, and—most importantly—to You. Amen

DAY 2

PUT GOD IN HIS RIGHTFUL PLACE

Do not have other gods besides Me.

Exodus 20:3 HCSB

As you think about the nature of your relationship with God, remember this: you will always have some type of relationship with Him—it is inevitable that your life must be lived in relationship to God. The question is not if you will have a relationship with Him; the burning question is whether that relationship will be one that seeks to honor Him . . . or not.

Are you willing to place God first in your life? And, are you willing to welcome Him into your heart? Unless you can honestly answer these questions with a resounding yes, then your relationship with God isn't what it could be or should be. Thankfully, God is always available, He's always ready to forgive, and He's waiting to hear from you now. The rest, of course, is up to you.

If God has the power to create and sustain the universe, He is more than able to sustain your marriage and your ministry, your faith and your finances, your hope and your health.

Anne Graham Lotz

It is when we come to the Lord in our nothingness, our powerlessness and our helplessness that He then enables us to love in a way which, without Him, would be absolutely impossible.

Elisabeth Elliot

TODAY'S PRAYER

Dear Lord, Your love is eternal and Your laws are everlasting. When I obey Your commandments, I am blessed. Today, I invite You to reign over every corner of my heart. I will have faith in You. I will sense Your presence; I will accept Your love; I will trust Your will; and I will praise You for the Savior of my life: Your Son Jesus. Amen

DAY 3

KEEP SEARCHING FOR WISDOM

*I will instruct you and show you the way to go;
with My eye on you, I will give counsel.*

Psalm 32:8 HCSB

Where will you find wisdom today? Will you seek it from God or from the world? As a thoughtful woman living in a society that is filled with temptations and distractions, you know that the world's brand of "wisdom" is everywhere . . . and it is dangerous. You live in a world where it's all too easy to stray far from the ultimate source of wisdom: God's Holy Word.

When you commit yourself to the daily study of God's Word—and when you live according to His commandments—you will become wise . . . in time. Today and every day, you should study His Word and live by it. When you do, you will accumulate a storehouse of wisdom that will enrich your own life and the lives of your family members, your friends, and the world.

If we neglect the Bible, we cannot expect to benefit from the wisdom and direction that result from knowing God's Word.

Vonette Bright

When you and I are related to Jesus Christ, our strength and wisdom and peace and joy and love and hope may run out, but His life rushes in to keep us filled to the brim. We are showered with blessings, not because of anything we have or have not done, but simply because of Him.

Anne Graham Lotz

TODAY'S PRAYER

Lord, make me a woman of wisdom and discernment. I seek wisdom, Lord, not as the world gives, but as You give. Lead me in Your ways and teach me from Your Word so that, in time, my wisdom might glorify Your kingdom and Your Son. Amen

DAY 4

WANT SPIRITUAL GROWTH? PRAY!

Rejoice in hope; be patient in affliction;
be persistent in prayer.
Romans 12:12 HCSB

In his letter, Paul advised members of the new church to "pray without ceasing." His advice applies to Christians of every generation. When we consult God on an hourly basis, we avail ourselves of His wisdom, His strength, and His love. As Corrie ten Boom observed, "Any concern that is too small to be turned into a prayer is too small to be made into a burden."

Today, instead of turning things over in your mind, turn them over to God in prayer. Instead of worrying about your next decision, ask God to lead the way. Don't limit your prayers to meals or bedtime. Become a woman of constant prayer. God is listening, and He wants to hear from you. Now.

Repentance removes old sins and wrong attitudes, and it opens the way for the Holy Spirit to restore our spiritual health.

Shirley Dobson

God gives us permission to forget our past and the understanding to live our present. He said He will remember our sins no more. (Psalm 103: 11-12)

Serita Ann Jakes

God specializes in things fresh and firsthand. His plans for you this year may outshine those of the past. He's prepared to fill your days with reasons to give Him praise.

Joni Eareckson Tada

TODAY'S PRAYER

Dear Lord, make me a woman of constant prayer. Your Holy Word commands me to pray without ceasing. In all things great and small, at all times, whether happy or sad, let me seek Your wisdom and Your strength . . . in prayer. Amen

STUDY HIS WORD

You will be a good servant of Christ Jesus,
nourished by the words of the faith
and of the good teaching that you have followed.
1 Timothy 4:6 HCSB

God's Word is unlike any other book. The Bible is a roadmap for life here on earth and for life eternal. As Christians, we are called upon to study God's Holy Word, to trust its promises, to follow its commandments, and to share its Good News with the world.

As women who seek to follow in the footsteps of the One from Galilee, we must study the Bible and meditate upon its meaning for our lives. Otherwise, we deprive ourselves of a priceless gift from our Creator. God's Holy Word is, indeed, a transforming, life-changing, one-of-a-kind treasure. And, a passing acquaintance with the Good Book is insufficient for Christians who seek to obey God's Word and to understand His will.

Weave the unveiling fabric of God's word through your heart and mind. It will hold strong, even if the rest of life unravels.

Gigi Graham Tchividjian

God can see clearly no matter how dark or foggy the night is. Trust His Word to guide you safely home.

Lisa Whelchel

The Bible became a living book and a guide for my life.

Vonette Bright

TODAY'S PRAYER

Dear Lord, the Bible is Your gift to me; let me use it. When I stray from Your Holy Word, Lord, I suffer. But, when I place Your Word at the very center of my life, I am blessed. Make me a faithful student of Your Word so that I might be a faithful servant in Your world every day. Amen

ENTRUSTING YOUR HOPES TO GOD

*You, Lord, give true peace to those who depend
on you, because they trust you.*

Isaiah 26:3 NCV

As every woman knows, hope is a perishable commodity. Despite God's promises, despite Christ's love, and despite our countless blessings, we frail human beings can still lose hope from time to time. When we do, we need the encouragement of Christian friends, the life-changing power of prayer, and the healing truth of God's Holy Word. If we find ourselves falling into the spiritual traps of worry and discouragement, we should seek the healing touch of Jesus and the encouraging words of fellow Christians. Even though this world can be a place of trials and struggles, God has promised us peace, joy, and eternal life if we give ourselves to Him.

Never yield to gloomy anticipation. Place your hope and confidence in God. He has no record of failure.

Mrs. Charles E. Cowman

I discovered that sorrow was not to be feared but rather endured with hope and expectancy that God would use it to visit and bless my life.

Jill Briscoe

Hope looks for the good in people, opens doors for people, discovers what can be done to help, lights a candle, does not yield to cynicism. Hope sets people free.

Barbara Johnson

TODAY'S PRAYER

Dear Lord, I will place my hope in You. If I become discouraged, I will turn to You. If I am afraid, I will seek strength in You. In every aspect of my life, I will trust You. You are my Father, and I will place my hope, my trust, and my faith in You. Amen

DAY 7

CHOOSING TO
PERSEVERE

But thanks be to God, who gives us the victory
through our Lord Jesus Christ. Therefore,
my beloved brethren, be steadfast, immovable,
always abounding in the work of the Lord,
knowing that your labor is not in vain in the Lord.
1 Corinthians 15:57-58 NKJV

A well-lived life is like a marathon, not a sprint—it calls for preparation, determination, and, of course, lots of perseverance. As an example of perfect perseverance, we Christians need look no further than Jesus.

Jesus finished what He began. Despite His suffering and despite the shame of the cross, Jesus was steadfast in His faithfulness to God. We, too, must remain faithful, especially during times of hardship. Sometimes, God may answer our prayers with silence, and when He does, we must patiently persevere. Remember this: whatever your problem, God can handle it.

Failure is one of life's most powerful teachers. How we handle our failures determines whether we're going to simply "get by" in life or "press on."

Beth Moore

Instead of being frustrated and overwhelmed by all that is going on in our world, go to the Lord and ask Him to give you His eternal perspective.

Kay Arthur

Every achievement worth remembering is stained with the blood of diligence and scarred by the wounds of disappointment.

Charles Swindoll

TODAY'S PRAYER

Lord, when life is difficult, I am tempted to abandon hope in the future. But You are my God, and I can draw strength from You. Let me trust You, Father, in good times and in bad times. Let me persevere—even if my soul is troubled—and let me follow Your Son, Jesus Christ, this day and forever. Amen

DAY 8

THE QUICKSAND OF BITTERNESS

Hatred stirs up conflicts, but love covers all offenses.
Proverbs 10:12 HCSB

Are you mired in the quicksand of bitterness or regret? If so, it's time to free yourself from the mire. The world holds few if any rewards for those who remain angrily focused upon the past. Still, the act of forgiveness is difficult for all but the most saintly people.

Being frail, fallible, imperfect human beings, most of us are quick to anger, quick to blame, slow to forgive, and even slower to forget. Yet we know that it's best to forgive others, just as we, too, have been forgiven.

If there exists even one person—including yourself—against whom you still harbor bitter feelings, it's time to forgive and move on. Bitterness, and regret are not part of God's plan for you, but God won't force you to forgive others. It's a job that only you can finish, and the sooner you finish it, the better.

Bitterness is a spiritual cancer, a rapidly growing malignancy that can consume your life. Bitterness cannot be ignored but must be healed at the very core, and only Christ can heal bitterness.

Beth Moore

Grudges are like hand grenades; it is wise to release them before they destroy you.

Barbara Johnson

Sin is any deed or memory that hampers or binds human personality.

Catherine Marshall

TODAY'S PRAYER

Heavenly Father, free me from anger and bitterness. When I am angry, I cannot feel the peace that You intend for my life. When I am bitter, I cannot sense Your presence. Keep me mindful that forgiveness is Your commandment. Let me turn away from bitterness and instead claim the spiritual abundance that You offer through the gift of Your Son. Amen

23

DAY 9

MAKING GOD'S PRIORITIES YOURS

Draw near to God, and He will draw near to you.
James 4:8 HCSB

Have you fervently asked God to help prioritize your life? Have you asked Him for guidance and for the courage to do the things that you know need to be done? If so, then you're continually inviting your Creator to reveal Himself in a variety of ways. As a follower of Christ, you must do no less.

When you make God's priorities your priorities, you will receive God's abundance and His peace. When you make God a full partner in every aspect of your life, He will lead you along the proper path: His path. When you allow God to reign over your heart, He will honor you with spiritual blessings that are simply too numerous to count. So, as you plan for the day ahead, make God's will your ultimate priority. When you do, every other priority will have a tendency to fall neatly into place.

How important it is for us—young and old—to live as if Jesus would return any day—to set our goals, make our choices, raise our children, and conduct business with the perspective of the imminent return of our Lord.

Gloria Gaither

Whatever you love most, be it sports, pleasure, business or God, that is your god.

Billy Graham

The essence of the Christian life is Jesus: that in all things He might have the preeminence, not that in some things He might have a place.

Franklin Graham

TODAY'S PRAYER

Lord, let Your priorities be my priorities. Let Your will be my will. Let Your Word be my guide, and let me grow in faith and in wisdom this day and every day. Amen

BE GENEROUS

*Each person should do as he has decided in
his heart—not out of regret or out of necessity,
for God loves a cheerful giver.*
2 Corinthians 9:7 HCSB

Do you want to improve your self-esteem?
Then make sure that you're a generous
person. When you give generously to
those who need your help, God will bless your
endeavors and enrich your life. So, if you're looking for a surefire way to improve the quality of
your day or your life, here it is: find ways to share
your blessings.

God rewards generosity just as surely as He
punishes sin. If we become generous disciples in
the service of our Lord, God blesses us in ways
that we cannot fully understand. But if we allow ourselves to become closefisted and miserly,
either with our possessions or with our love, we
deprive ourselves of the spiritual abundance that
would otherwise be ours.

The measure of a life, after all, is not its duration but its donation.

Corrie ten Boom

As faithful stewards of what we have, ought we not to give earnest thought to our staggering surplus?

Elisabeth Elliot

When somebody needs a helping hand, he doesn't need it tomorrow or the next day. He needs it now, and that's exactly when you should offer to help. Good deeds, if they are really good, happen sooner rather than later.

Marie T. Freeman

TODAY'S PRAYER

Dear Lord, Your Word tells me that it is more blessed to give than to receive. Make me a faithful steward of the gifts You have given me, and let me share those gifts generously with others, today and every day that I live. Amen

DAY 11

SEEK FELLOWSHIP

Then all the people began to eat and drink,
send portions, and have a great celebration,
because they had understood
the words that were explained to them.
Nehemiah 8:12 HCSB

Fellowship with other believers should be an integral part of your life. Your association with fellow Christians should be uplifting, enlightening, encouraging, and consistent.

Are you an active member of your own fellowship? Are you a builder of bridges inside the four walls of your church and outside it? Do you contribute to God's glory by contributing your time and your talents to a close-knit band of believers? Hopefully so. The fellowship of believers is intended to be a powerful tool for spreading God's Good News and uplifting His children. And God intends for you to be a fully contributing member of that fellowship. Your intentions should be the same.

Be united with other Christians. A wall with loose bricks is not good. The bricks must be cemented together.

Corrie ten Boom

When many men rejoice together, there is a richer job in each individual, since they enkindle themselves and they inflame one another.

St. Augustine

Christian brotherhood is not an ideal which we must realize; it is rather a reality created by God in Christ in which we may participate.

Dietrich Bonhoeffer

TODAY'S PRAYER

Heavenly Father, You have given me a community of supporters called the church. Let our fellowship be a reflection of the love we feel for each other and the love we feel for You. Amen

THE GOOD NEWS

*Grace to you and peace from God our Father
and the Lord Jesus Christ.*
Philippians 1:2 HCSB

God's grace is not earned . . . thank goodness! To earn God's love and His gift of eternal life would be far beyond the abilities of even the most righteous man or woman. Thankfully, grace is not an earthly reward for righteous behavior; it is a blessed spiritual gift which can be accepted by believers who dedicate themselves to God through Christ. When we accept Christ into our hearts, we are saved by His grace.

God's grace is the ultimate gift, and we owe to Him the ultimate in thanksgiving. Let us praise the Creator for His priceless gift, and let us share the Good News with all who cross our paths. We return our Father's love by accepting His grace and by sharing His message and His love. When we do, we are eternally blessed.

God does what few men can do—forgets the sins of others.

Anonymous

Forgiveness is God's command.

Martin Luther

God forgets the past. Imitate him.

Max Lucado

When God forgives, He forgets. He buries our sins in the sea and puts a sign on the shore saying, "No Fishing Allowed."

Corrie ten Boom

TODAY'S PRAYER

Dear Lord, I have fallen short of Your commandments, and You have forgiven me. You have blessed me with Your love and Your mercy. Enable me to be merciful toward others, Father, just as You have been merciful to me, and let me share Your love with all whom I meet. Amen

DAY 13

DO FIRST THINGS FIRST

Therefore, get your minds ready for action,
being self-disciplined . . . .
1 Peter 1:13 HCSB

First things first. These words are easy to speak but hard to put into practice. For busy women living in a demanding world, placing first things first can be difficult indeed. Why? Because so many people are expecting so many things from us!

If you're having trouble prioritizing your day, perhaps you've been trying to organize your life according to your own plans, not God's. A better strategy, of course, is to take your daily obligations and place them in the hands of the One who created you. To do so, you must prioritize your day according to God's commandments, and you must seek His will and His wisdom in all matters. Then, you can face the day with the assurance that the same God who created our universe out of nothingness will help you place first things first in your own life.

Have you prayed about your resources lately? Find out how God wants you to use your time and your money. No matter what it costs, forsake all that is not of God.

Kay Arthur

There were endless demands on Jesus' time. Still he was able to make that amazing claim of "completing the work you gave me to do." (John 17:4 NIV)

Elisabeth Elliot

Let's face it. None of us can do a thousand things to the glory of God. And, in our own vain attempt to do so, we stand the risk of forfeiting a precious thing.

Beth Moore

TODAY'S PRAYER

Dear Lord, today is a new day. Help me finish the important tasks first, even if those tasks are unpleasant. Don't let me put off until tomorrow what I should do today. Amen

DAY 14

PRAY FOR PERSPECTIVE

So if you have been raised with the Messiah,
seek what is above, where the Messiah is,
seated at the right hand of God.
Colossians 3:1 HCSB

If a temporary loss of perspective has left you worried, exhausted, or both, it's time to readjust your thought patterns. Negative thoughts are habit-forming; thankfully, so are positive ones. With practice, you can form the habit of focusing on God's priorities and your own possibilities. When you do, you'll soon discover that you will spend less time fretting about your challenges and more time praising God for His gifts.

When you call upon the Lord and prayerfully seek His will, He will give you wisdom and perspective. When you make God's priorities your priorities, He will direct your steps and calm your fears. So today and every day hereafter, pray for a sense of balance and perspective. And remember: no problems are too big for God.

Attitude is the mind's paintbrush; it can color any situation.

Barbara Johnson

Instead of being frustrated and overwhelmed by all that is going on in our world, go to the Lord and ask Him to give you His eternal perspective.

Kay Arthur

The proper perspective creates within us a spirit of reaching outside of ourselves with joy and enthusiasm.

Luci Swindoll

TODAY'S PRAYER

Dear Lord, give me wisdom and perspective. Guide me according to Your plans for my life and according to Your commandments. And keep me mindful, Dear Lord, that Your truth is—and will forever be—the ultimate truth. Amen

VERY BIG PLANS

Teach me to do Your will, for You are my God.
May Your gracious Spirit lead me on level ground.

Psalm 143:10 HCSB

God has plans for your life, but He won't force His plans upon you. Your Creator has given you the ability to make decisions on your own. With that freedom comes the responsibility of living with the consequences of your choices.

If you seek to live in accordance with God's plan for your life, you will study His Word, you will be attentive to His instructions, and you will be watchful for His signs. You will associate with fellow believers who, by their words and actions, will encourage your own spiritual growth. You will assiduously avoid those two terrible temptations: the temptation to sin and the temptation to squander time. And finally, you will listen carefully, even reverently, to the conscience that God has placed in your heart.

When the dream of our heart is one that God has planted there, a strange happiness flows into us. At that moment, all of the spiritual resources of the universe are released to help us. Our praying is then at one with the will of God and becomes a channel for the Creator's purposes for us and our world.

Catherine Marshall

Let's never forget that some of God's greatest mercies are His refusals. He says no in order that He may, in some way we cannot imagine, say yes. All His ways with us are merciful. His meaning is always love.

Elisabeth Elliot

TODAY'S PRAYER

Dear Lord, I am Your creation, and You created me for a reason. Give me the wisdom to follow Your direction for my life's journey. Let me do Your work here on earth by seeking Your will and living it, knowing that when I trust in You, Father, I am eternally blessed. Amen

DAY 16

DO YOU BELIEVE IN MIRACLES?

You are the God who works wonders;
You revealed Your strength among the peoples.
Psalm 77:14 HCSB

If you haven't seen any of God's miracles lately, you haven't been looking. Throughout history the Creator has intervened in the course of human events in ways that cannot be explained by science or human rationale. And He's still doing so today.

God's miracles are not limited to special occasions, nor are they witnessed by a select few. God is crafting His wonders all around us: the miracle of the birth of a new baby; the miracle of a world renewing itself with every sunrise; the miracle of lives transformed by God's love and grace. Each day, God's handiwork is evident for all to see and experiences, so keep your eyes and your heart open. Be watchful, and you'll soon be amazed.

When we face an impossible situation, all self-reliance and self-confidence must melt away; we must be totally dependent on Him for the resources.

Anne Graham Lotz

Faith means believing in realities that go beyond sense and sight. It is the awareness of unseen divine realities all around you.

Joni Eareckson Tada

TODAY'S PRAYER

Dear God, nothing is impossible for You. Your infinite power is beyond human understanding—keep me always mindful of Your strength. When I lose hope, give me faith; when others lose hope, let me tell them of Your glory and Your works. Today, Lord, let me expect the miraculous, and let me trust in You. Amen

SPEND TIME WITH GOD

But have nothing to do with irreverent and silly myths. Rather, train yourself in godliness.

1 Timothy 4:7 HCSB

Each new day is a gift from God, and if we are wise, we spend a few quiet moments each morning thanking the Giver. Daily life is woven together with the threads of habit, and no habit is more important to our spiritual health than the discipline of daily prayer and devotion to the Creator.

When we begin each day with heads bowed and hearts lifted, we remind ourselves of God's love, His protection, and His commandments. And if we are wise, we align our priorities for the coming day with the teachings and commandments that God has given us through His Word.

Are you seeking to change some aspect of your life? Do you seek to improve the condition of your spiritual or physical health? If so, ask for God's help and ask for it many times each day . . . starting with your morning devotional.

Jesus challenges you and me to keep our focus daily on the cross of His will if we want to be His disciples.

Anne Graham Lotz

I suggest you discipline yourself to spend time daily in a systematic reading of God's Word. Make this "quiet time" a priority that nobody can change.

Warren Wiersbe

A person with no devotional life generally struggles with faith and obedience.

Charles Stanley

TODAY'S PRAYER

Dear Lord, every day of my life is a journey with You. I will take time today to think, to pray, and to study Your Word. Guide my steps, Father, and keep me mindful that today offers yet another opportunity to celebrate Your blessings, Your love, and Your Son. Amen

BE A JOYFUL CHRISTIAN

Make me hear joy and gladness.
Psalm 51:8 NKJV

Barbara Johnson says, "You have to look for the joy. Look for the light of God that is hitting your life, and you will find sparkles you didn't know were there."

Have you experienced that kind of joy? Hopefully so, because it's not enough to hear someone else talk about being joyful—you must actually experience that kind of joy in order to understand it.

Should you expect to be a joy-filled woman 24 hours a day, seven days a week, from this moment on? No. But you can (and should) experience pockets of joy frequently—that's the kind of joy-filled life that a woman like you deserves to live.

What is your focus today? Joy comes when it is Jesus first, others second . . . then you.

Kay Arthur

The Christian lifestyle is not one of legalistic do's and don'ts, but one that is positive, attractive, and joyful.

Vonette Bright

If you're a thinking Christian, you will be a joyful Christian.

Marie T. Freeman

There may be no trumpet sound or loud applause when we make a right decision, just a calm sense of resolution and peace.

Gloria Gaither

Today's Prayer

Dear Lord, You have given me so many blessings, starting with my family. I will keep joy in my heart as I thank You, Lord, for every single blessing You've given me. Amen

FORGIVE EVERYBODY

For if you forgive people their wrongdoing,
your heavenly Father will forgive you as well.
But if you don't forgive people,
your Father will not forgive your wrongdoing.
Matthew 6:14-15 HCSB

The world holds few if any rewards for those who remain angrily focused upon the past. Still, the act of forgiveness is difficult for all but the most saintly men and women. Are you mired in the quicksand of hatred or regret? If so, you are not only disobeying God's Word, you are also wasting your time.

Being frail, fallible, imperfect human beings, most of us are quick to anger, quick to blame, slow to forgive, and even slower to forget. Yet as Christians, we are commanded to forgive others, just as we, too, have been forgiven.

If there exists even one person—alive or dead—against whom you hold bitter feelings, it's time to forgive. Hatred, bitterness, and regret are not part of God's plan for your life. Forgiveness is.

The fact is, God no longer deals with us in judgment but in mercy. If people got what they deserved, this old planet would have ripped apart at the seams centuries ago. Praise God that because of His great love "we are not consumed, for his compassions never fail" (Lam. 3:22).

Joni Eareckson Tada

God expects us to forgive others as He has forgiven us; we are to follow His example by having a forgiving heart.

Vonette Bright

The more you practice the art of forgiving, the quicker you'll master the art of living.

Marie T. Freeman

TODAY'S PRAYER

Dear Lord, let forgiveness rule my heart, even when forgiveness is difficult. Let me be Your obedient servant, Lord, and let me be a woman who forgives others just as You have forgiven me. Amen

FOLLOW YOUR CONSCIENCE

*Let us draw near with a true heart in full assurance
of faith, our hearts sprinkled clean from an evil
conscience and our bodies washed in pure water.*

Hebrews 10:22 HCSB

God gave you a conscience for a very good reason: to make your path conform to His will. Billy Graham observed, "Most of us follow our conscience as we follow a wheelbarrow. We push it in front of us in the direction we want to go." To do so, of course, is a profound mistake. Yet all of us, on occasion, have failed to listen to the voice that God planted in our hearts, and all of us have suffered the consequences.

Wise believers make it a practice to listen carefully to that quiet internal voice. Count yourself among that number. When your conscience speaks, listen and learn. In all likelihood, God is trying to get His message through. And in all likelihood, it is a message that you desperately need to hear.

God desires that we become spiritually healthy enough through faith to have a conscience that rightly interprets the work of the Holy Spirit.

Beth Moore

My conscience is captive to the word of God.

Martin Luther

Guilt is a healthy regret for telling God one thing and doing another.

Max Lucado

TODAY'S PRAYER

Dear Lord, You speak to me through the Bible, through teachers, and through friends. And, Father, You speak to me through that still, small voice that warns me when I stray from Your will. In these quiet moments and throughout the day, show me Your plan for my life, Lord, that I might serve You. Amen

DAY 21

TOO MANY DISTRACTIONS?

Keep your eyes on Jesus, who both began and
finished this race we're in. Study how he did it.
Because he never lost sight of where he was headed,
that exhilarating finish in and with God, he could
put up with anything along the way:
cross, shame, whatever. And now he's there,
in the place of honor, right alongside God.

Hebrews 12:2 MSG

All of us must live through those days when the traffic jams, the computer crashes, and the coffee spills. But, when we find ourselves distracted by the minor frustrations of life, we must catch ourselves, take a deep breath, and lift our thoughts upward.

Although we may, at times, struggle mightily to rise above the distractions of life, we need never struggle alone. God is here—eternal and faithful, with infinite patience and love—and, if we reach out to Him, He will restore our sense of perspective and give peace to our souls.

Give me the person who says, "This one thing I do, and not these fifty things I dabble in."

D. L. Moody

The demand of every day kept me so busy that I subconsciously equated my busyness with commitment to Christ.

Vonette Bright

You can't get second things by putting them first; you can get second things only by putting first things first.

C. S. Lewis

TODAY'S PRAYER

Dear Lord, give me the wisdom to focus, not on the distractions of the moment, but on the priorities that matter. Today and every day, Father, guide my thoughts and guard my heart. Amen

JESUS WAS A SERVANT (YOU MUST BE, TOO)

*Be strong and of good courage, and do it;
do not fear nor be dismayed, for the Lord God—
my God—will be with you. He will not leave you
nor forsake you, until you have finished all the work
for the service of the house of the Lord.*

1 Chronicles 28:20 NKJV

Jesus teaches that the most esteemed men and women are not the self-congratulatory leaders of society but are instead the humblest of servants. But, we sometimes fall short as we seek to puff ourselves up and glorify our own accomplishments. To do so is wrong.

As a humble servant, you will glorify yourself, not before men, but before God, and that's what God intends. After all, earthly glory is fleeting: here today and all too soon gone. But, heavenly glory endures throughout eternity. So, the choice is yours: Either you can lift yourself up here on earth and be humbled in heaven, or vice versa.

God wants us to serve Him with a willing spirit, one that would choose no other way.

Beth Moore

In the very place where God has put us, whatever its limitations, whatever kind of work it may be, we may indeed serve the Lord Christ.

Elisabeth Elliot

Doing something positive toward another person is a practical approach to feeling good about yourself.

Barbara Johnson

TODAY'S PRAYER

Dear Lord, in weak moments, we may try to build ourselves up by placing ourselves ahead of others. But You want us to be humble servants to those who need our encouragement, our help, and our love. Today, we will do our best to follow in the footsteps of Your Son Jesus by serving others humbly, faithfully, and lovingly. Amen

DAY 23

GETTING IT DONE NOW

When you make a vow to God, don't delay
fulfilling it, because He does not delight in fools.
Fulfill what you vow.
Ecclesiastes 5:4 HCSB

The old saying is both familiar and true: actions speak louder than words. And as believers, we must beware: our actions should always give credence to the changes that Christ can make in the lives of those who walk with Him.

God calls upon each of us to act in accordance with His will and with respect for His commandments. If we are to be responsible believers, we must realize that it is never enough simply to hear the instructions of God; we must also live by them. And it is never enough to wait idly by while others do God's work here on earth; we, too, must act. Doing God's work is a responsibility that each of us must bear, and when we do, our loving Heavenly Father rewards our efforts with a bountiful harvest.

We spend our lives dreaming of the future, not realizing that a little of it slips away every day.

Barbara Johnson

God has lots of folks who intend to go to work for him "some day." What He needs is more people who are willing to work for Him this day.

Marie T. Freeman

Logic will not change an emotion, but action will.

Zig Ziglar

TODAY'S PRAYER

Dear Lord, I have heard Your Word, and I have felt Your presence in my heart; let me act accordingly. Let my words and deeds serve as a testimony to the changes You have made in my life. Let me praise You, Father, by following in the footsteps of Your Son, and let others see Him through me. Amen

DAY 24

A PRACTICAL CHRISTIAN

*Pure and undefiled religion before our God and
Father is this: to look after orphans and
widows in their distress and to keep oneself
unstained by the world.*
James 1:27 HCSB

What is "real" Christianity? Think of it as an ongoing relationship—an all-encompassing relationship with God and with His Son Jesus. It is inevitable that your life must be lived in relationship to God. The question is not if you will have a relationship with Him; the burning question is whether that relationship will be one that seeks to honor Him or one that seeks to ignore Him.

We live in a world that discourages heartfelt devotion and obedience to God. Everywhere we turn, we are confronted by a mind-numbing assortment of distractions. Yet even on our busiest days, God beckons us to slow down and consult Him. When we do, we avail ourselves of the peace and abundance that only He can give.

The Christian lifestyle is not one of legalistic do's and don'ts, but one that is positive, attractive, and joyful.

Vonette Bright

As you walk by faith, you live a righteous life, for righteousness is always by faith.

Kay Arthur

This life of faith, then, consists in just this—being a child in the Father's house. Let the ways of childish confidence and freedom from care, which so please you and win your heart when you observe your own little ones, teach you what you should be in your attitude toward God.

Hannah Whitall Smith

TODAY'S PRAYER

Dear Lord, today, I will choose to please You and only You. I will obey Your commandments, and I will praise You for Your gifts, for Your love, and for Your Son. Amen

DAY 25

CONSIDERING THE CROSS

But God forbid that I should boast except in the cross of our Lord Jesus Christ, by whom the world has been crucified to me, and I to the world.

Galatians 6:14 NKJV

As we consider Christ's sacrifice on the cross, we should be profoundly humbled and profoundly grateful. And today, as we come to Christ in prayer, we should do so in a spirit of quiet, heartfelt devotion to the One who gave His life so that we might have life eternal.

He was the Son of God, but He wore a crown of thorns. He was the Savior of mankind, yet He was put to death on the cross. He offered His healing touch to an unsaved world, and yet the same hands that had healed the sick and raised the dead were pierced with nails.

Christ has offered to walk with you through this life and throughout all eternity. As you approach Him today in prayer, think about His sacrifice and His grace. And be humble.

God is my heavenly Father. He loves me with an everlasting love. The proof of that is the Cross.

Elisabeth Elliot

The cross takes care of the past. The cross takes care of the flesh. The cross takes care of the world.

Kay Arthur

The heaviest end of the cross lies ever on His shoulders. If He bids us carry a burden, He carries it also.

C. H. Spurgeon

TODAY'S PRAYER

Dear Jesus, You are my Savior and my protector. You suffered on the cross for me, and I will give You honor and praise every day of my life. I will honor You with my words, my thoughts, and my prayers. And I will live according to Your commandments, so that through me, others might come to know Your perfect love. Amen

DON'T BE ENVIOUS

*Let us walk properly, as in the day, not in revelry
and drunkenness, not in lewdness and lust,
not in strife and envy.*
Romans 13:13 NKJV

I n a competitive, cut-throat world, it is easy to become envious of other's success. But it's wrong.

We know intuitively that envy is wrong, but because we are frail, imperfect human beings, we may find ourselves struggling with feelings of envy or resentment, or both. These feelings may be especially forceful when we see other people experience unusually good fortune.

Have you recently felt the pangs of envy creeping into your heart? If so, it's time to focus on the marvelous things that God has done for you and your family. And just as importantly, you must refrain from preoccupying yourself with the blessings that God has chosen to give others.

Discontent dries up the soul.

Elisabeth Elliot

What God asks, does, or requires of others is not my business; it is His.

Kay Arthur

We might occasionally be able to change our circumstances, but only God can change our hearts.

Beth Moore

Too many Christians envy the sinners their pleasure and the saints their joy because they don't have either one.

Martin Luther

TODAY'S PRAYER

Dear Lord, deliver me from the needless pain of envy. You have given me countless blessings. Let me be thankful for the gifts I have received, and let me never be resentful of the gifts You have given others. Amen

CONTROL YOUR TEMPER

Don't let the sun go down on your anger,
and don't give the Devil an opportunity.
Ephesians 4:26-27 HCSB

Sometimes, anger is appropriate. Even Jesus became angry when confronted with the moneychangers in the temple. On occasion, you, like Jesus, will confront evil, and when you do, you may respond as He did: vigorously and without reservation. But, more often than not, your frustrations will be of the more mundane variety. As long as you live here on earth, you will face countless opportunities to lose your temper over small, relatively insignificant events: a traffic jam, a spilled cup of coffee, an inconsiderate comment, a broken promise. When you are tempted to lose your temper over the minor inconveniences of life, don't. Turn away from anger, hatred, bitterness, and regret. Turn instead to God.

Life is too short to spend it being angry, bored, or dull.

Barbara Johnson

If your temper gets the best of you . . . then other people get to see the worst in you.

Marie T. Freeman

Anger unresolved will only bring you woe.

Kay Arthur

Anger breeds remorse in the heart, discord in the home, bitterness in the community, and confusion in the state.

Billy Graham

TODAY'S PRAYER

Dear Lord, help me to turn away from angry thoughts. Help me always to use Jesus as my guide for life, and let me trust His promises today and forever. Amen

DAY 28

YOU'D BETTER BEWARE

The good obtain favor from the Lord,
but He condemns a man who schemes.
Proverbs 12:2 HCSB

This world is God's creation, and it contains the wonderful fruits of His handiwork. But, the world also contains countless opportunities to stray from God's will. Temptations are everywhere, and the devil, it seems, never takes a day off. Our task, as believers, is to turn away from temptation and to place our lives squarely in the center of God's will.

In his letter to Jewish Christians, Peter offered a stern warning: "Your adversary, the devil, prowls around like a roaring lion, seeking someone to devour" (1 Peter 5:8 NASB). What was true in New Testament times is equally true in our own. Evil is indeed abroad in the world, and Satan continues to sow the seeds of destruction far and wide. As Christians, we must guard our hearts by earnestly wrapping ourselves in the protection of God's Holy Word.

Where God's ministers are most successful, there the powers of darkness marshal their forces for the conflict.

Lottie Moon

We are in a continual battle with the spiritual forces of evil, but we will triumph when we yield to God's leading and call on His powerful presence in prayer.

Shirley Dobson

God judged it better to bring good out of evil than to suffer no evil to exist.

St. Augustine

TODAY'S PRAYER

Dear Lord, because You have given Your children free will, the world is a place where evil threatens our lives and our souls. Protect us, Father, from the evils and temptations of this difficult age. Help us to trust You, Father, and to obey Your Word, knowing that Your ultimate victory over evil is both inevitable and complete. Amen

THE WISDOM TO BE GENEROUS

Freely you have received, freely give.
Matthew 10:8 NKJV

The thread of generosity is woven—completely and inextricably—into the very fabric of Christ's teachings. As He sent His disciples out to heal the sick and spread God's message of salvation, Jesus offered this guiding principle: "Freely you have received, freely give" (Matthew 10:8 NIV). The principle still applies. If we are to be disciples of Christ, we must give freely of our time, our possessions, and our love.

Today, make this pledge and keep it: Be a cheerful, generous, courageous giver. The world needs your help, and you need the spiritual rewards that will be yours when you share your possessions, your talents, and your time.

What is your focus today? Joy comes when it is Jesus first, others second . . . then you.

Kay Arthur

We can't do everything, but can we do anything more valuable than invest ourselves in another?

Elisabeth Elliot

The measure of a life, after all, is not its duration but its donation.

Corrie ten Boom

All kindness and good deeds, we must keep silent. The result will be an inner reservoir of power.

Catherine Marshall

TODAY'S PRAYER

Father, Your gifts are priceless. You gave Your Son Jesus to save us, and Your motivation was love. I pray that the gifts I give to others will come from an overflow of my heart, and that they will echo the great love You have for all of Your children. Amen

DAY 30

CONTAGIOUS CHRISTIANITY

*Therefore, everyone who will acknowledge
Me before men, I will also acknowledge him
before My Father in heaven.*
Matthew 10:32 HCSB

Genuine, heartfelt Christianity can be highly contagious. When you've experienced the transforming power of God's love, you feel the need to share the Good News of His only begotten Son. So, whether you realize it or not, you can be sure that you are being led to share the story of your faith with family, with friends, and with the world.

Today, don't be bashful or timid: Talk about Jesus and, while you're at it, show the world what it really means to follow Him. After all, the fields are ripe for the harvest, time is short, and the workers are surprisingly few. So please share your story today because tomorrow may indeed be too late.

To be a Christian means to forgive the inexcusable, because God has forgiven the inexcusable in you.

C. S. Lewis

The Holy Spirit testifies of Jesus. So when you are filled with the Holy Spirit, you speak about our Lord and really live to His honor.

Corrie ten Boom

Going to church does not make you a Christian anymore than going to McDonalds makes you a hamburger.

Anonymous

TODAY'S PRAYER

Thank You, Lord, for Your Son. His love is boundless, infinite, and eternal. Today, let me pause and reflect upon Christ's love for me, and let me share that love with all those who cross my path. And, as an expression of my love for Him, let me share Christ's saving message with a world that desperately needs His grace. Amen

DAY 31

GUARD YOUR HEART

*Finally, brethren, whatever things are true,
whatever things are noble, whatever things are just,
whatever things are pure, whatever things are lovely,
whatever things are of good report,
if there is any virtue and if there is anything
praiseworthy—meditate on these things.*

Philippians 4:8 NKJV

You are near and dear to God. He loves you more than you can imagine, and He wants the very best for you. And one more thing: God wants you to guard your heart.

Every day, you are faced with choices. You can do the right thing, or not. You can be prudent, or not. You can be kind, and generous, and obedient to God. Or not.

Today, the world will offer you countless opportunities to let down your guard and, by doing so, make needless mistakes that may injure you or your loved ones. So be watchful and obedient. Guard your heart by giving it to your Heavenly Father; it is safe with Him.

Becoming pure is a process of spiritual growth, and taking seriously the confession of sin during prayer time moves that process along, causing us to purge our life of practices that displease God.

Elizabeth George

Holiness has never been the driving force of the majority. It is, however, mandatory for anyone who wants to enter the kingdom.

Elisabeth Elliot

He doesn't need an abundance of words. He doesn't need a dissertation about your life. He just wants your attention. He wants your heart.

Kathy Troccoli

TODAY'S PRAYER

Dear Lord, I will guard my heart against the evils, the temptations, and the distractions of this world. I will focus, instead, upon Your love, Your blessings, and Your Son. Amen

CHOOSING INTEGRITY

A good name is to be chosen over great wealth.
Proverbs 22:1 HCSB

Honesty is the best policy, but it is not always the easiest policy. Sometimes, the truth hurts, and sometimes, it's tough to be a woman of integrity . . . tough, but essential.

Charles Swindoll correctly observed, "Nothing speaks louder or more powerfully than a life of integrity." Godly women agree.

Integrity is built slowly over a lifetime. It is the sum of every right decision and every honest word. It is forged on the anvil of honorable work and polished by the twin virtues of honesty and fairness. Integrity is a precious thing—difficult to build but easy to tear down. As believers in Christ, we must seek to live each day with discipline, honesty, and faith. When we do, integrity becomes a habit. And God smiles.

The single most important element in any human relationship is honesty—with oneself, with God, and with others.

Catherine Marshall

The commandment of absolute truthfulness is really only another name for the fullness of discipleship.

Dietrich Bonhoeffer

Much guilt arises in the life of the believer from practicing the chameleon life of environmental adaptation.

Beth Moore

TODAY'S PRAYER

Dear Lord, You search my heart and know me far better than I know myself. May I be Your worthy servant, and may I live according to Your commandments. Let me be a woman of integrity, Lord, and let my words and deeds be a testimony to You, today and always. Amen

PASSIONATE ABOUT YOUR PATH

*Don't work only while being watched,
in order to please men, but as slaves of Christ,
do God's will from your heart. Render service with
a good attitude, as to the Lord and not to men.*

Ephesians 6:6-7 HCSB

Do you see each day as a glorious opportunity to serve God and to do His will? Are you enthused about life, or do you struggle through each day giving scarcely a thought to God's blessings? Are you constantly praising God for His gifts, and are you sharing His Good News with the world? And are you excited about the possibilities for service that God has placed before you, whether at home, at work, at church, or at school? You should be.

You are the recipient of Christ's sacrificial love. Accept it enthusiastically and share it fervently. Jesus deserves your enthusiasm; the world deserves it; and you deserve the experience of sharing it.

Living life with a consistent spiritual walk deeply influences those we love most.

Vonette Bright

Your light is the truth of the Gospel message itself as well as your witness as to Who Jesus is and what He has done for you. Don't hide it.

Anne Graham Lotz

Making up a string of excuses is usually harder than doing the work.

Marie T. Freeman

Enthusiasm, like the flu, is contagious—we get it from one another.

Barbara Johnson

TODAY'S PRAYER

Dear Lord, I know that others are watching the way that I live my life. Help me to be an enthusiastic Christian with a faith that is contagious. Amen.

73

DAY 34

BE DISCIPLINED

But I discipline my body and bring it into subjection,
lest, when I have preached to others,
I myself should become disqualified.

1 Corinthians 9:27 NKJV

Wise women understand the importance of discipline. In Proverbs 28:19, the message is clear: "Those who work their land will have plenty of food, but the ones who chase empty dreams instead will end up poor" (NCV).

If we work diligently and faithfully, we can expect a bountiful harvest. But we must never expect the harvest to precede the labor.

Poet Mary Frances Butts advised, "Build a little fence of trust around today. Fill each space with loving work, and therein stay."

Thoughtful women understand that God doesn't reward laziness or misbehavior. To the contrary, God expects His children (of all ages) to lead disciplined lives . . . and when they do, He rewards them.

Personal humility is a spiritual discipline and the hallmark of the service of Jesus.

Franklin Graham

We set our eyes on the finish line, forgetting the past, and straining toward the mark of spiritual maturity and fruitfulness.

Vonette Bright

It's sobering to contemplate how much time, effort, sacrifice, compromise, and attention we give to acquiring and increasing our supply of something that is totally insignificant in eternity.

Anne Graham Lotz

TODAY'S PRAYER

Dear Lord, make me a woman of discipline and righteousness. Let my conduct show others what it means to be a faithful Christian, and let me follow Your will and Your Word, today and every day. Amen

DAY 35

TRUST GOD'S PROMISES

For you need endurance,
so that after you have done God's will,
you may receive what was promised.

Hebrews 10:36 HCSB

What do you expect from the day ahead? Are you expecting God to do wonderful things, or are you living beneath a cloud of doubt? The familiar words of Psalm 118:24 remind us of a profound yet simple truth: "This is the day which the LORD hath made; we will rejoice and be glad in it" (KJV).

For Christian believers, every day begins and ends with God's Son and God's promises. When we accept Christ into our hearts, God promises us the opportunity for earthly peace and spiritual abundance. But more importantly, God promises us the priceless gift of eternal life.

As we face the inevitable challenges of life, we must arm ourselves with the promises of God's Word. When we do, we can expect the best, not only for the day ahead, but also for all eternity.

Our future may look fearfully intimidating, yet we can look up to the Engineer of the Universe, confident that nothing escapes His attention or slips out of the control of those strong hands.

Elisabeth Elliot

Worries carry responsibilities that belong to God, not to you. Worry does not enable us to escape evil; it makes us unfit to cope with it when it comes.

Corrie ten Boom

God will never let you sink under your circumstances. He always provide a safety net and His love always encircles.

Barbara Johnson

TODAY'S PRAYER

Lord, Your Holy Word contains promises, and I will trust them. I will use the Bible as my guide, and I will trust You, Lord, to speak to me through Your Holy Spirit and through Your Holy Word, this day and forever. Amen

DAY 36

A HEALTHY FEAR OF GOD

Therefore, since we are receiving a kingdom that cannot be shaken, let us hold on to grace. By it, we may serve God acceptably, with reverence and awe.

Hebrews 12:28 HCSB

Are you a woman who possesses a healthy, fearful respect for God's power? Hopefully so. After all, God's Word teaches that the fear of the Lord is the beginning of knowledge (Proverbs 1:7).

When we fear the Creator—and when we honor Him by obeying His commandments—we receive God's approval and His blessings. But, when we ignore Him or disobey His commandments, we invite disastrous consequences.

God's hand shapes the universe, and it shapes our lives. God maintains absolute sovereignty over His creation, and His power is beyond comprehension. The fear of the Lord is, indeed, the beginning of knowledge. But thankfully, once we possess a healthy, reverent fear of God, we need never be fearful of anything else.

It is not possible that mortal men should be thoroughly conscious of the divine presence without being filled with awe.

C. H. Spurgeon

The remarkable thing about fearing God is that when you fear God, you fear nothing else, whereas if you do not fear God, you fear everything else.

Oswald Chambers

When true believers are awed by the greatness of God and by the privilege of becoming His children, then they become sincerely motivated, effective evangelists.

Bill Hybels

TODAY'S PRAYER

Dear Lord, let my greatest fear be the fear of displeasing You. I will strive, Father, to obey Your commandments and seek Your will this day and every day of my life. Amen

WHEN YOU HAVE DOUBTS

When I am filled with cares,
Your comfort brings me joy.
Psalm 94:19 HCSB

If you've never had any doubts about your faith, then you can stop reading this page now and skip to the next. But if you've ever been plagued by doubts about your faith or your God, keep reading.

Even some of the most faithful Christians are, at times, beset by occasional bouts of discouragement and doubt. But even when we feel far removed from God, God is never far removed from us. He is always with us, always willing to calm the storms of life—always willing to replace our doubts with comfort and assurance.

Whenever you're plagued by doubts, that's precisely the moment you should seek God's presence by genuinely seeking to establish a deeper, more meaningful relationship with His Son.

We are most vulnerable to the piercing winds of doubt when we distance ourselves from the mission and fellowship to which Christ has called us.

Joni Eareckson Tada

Fear and doubt are conquered by a faith that rejoices. And faith can rejoice because the promises of God are as certain as God Himself.

Kay Arthur

TODAY'S PRAYER

Dear God, sometimes this world can be a puzzling place, filled with uncertainty and doubt. When I am unsure of my next step, keep me mindful that You are always near and that You can overcome any challenge. Give me faith, Father, and let me remember always that with Your love and Your power, I can live courageously and faithfully today and every day. Amen

REMEMBER: YOU DON'T HAVE TO BE PERFECT

Those who wait for perfect weather will never plant seeds; those who look at every cloud will never harvest crops. Plant early in the morning, and work until evening, because you don't know if this or that will succeed. They might both do well.

Ecclesiastes 11:4, 6 NCV

Expectations, expectations, expectations! As a woman living in the 21st century, you know that demands can be high, and expectations even higher. The media delivers an endless stream of messages that tell you how to look, how to behave, how to eat, and how to dress. The media's expectations are impossible to meet—God's are not. God doesn't expect you to be perfect . . . and neither should you.

Remember: the expectations that really matter are God's expectations. Everything else takes a back seat. So do your best to please God, and don't worry too much about what others think.

God is so inconceivably good. He's not looking for perfection. He already saw it in Christ. He's looking for affection.

Beth Moore

The happiest people in the world are not those who have no problems, but the people who have learned to live with those things that are less than perfect.

James Dobson

The greatest destroyer of good works is the desire to do great works.

C. H. Spurgeon

TODAY'S PRAYER

Lord, this world has so many expectations of me, but today I will not seek to meet the world's expectations; I will do my best to meet Your expectations. I will make You my ultimate priority, Lord, by serving You, by praising You, by loving You, and by obeying You. Amen

STEWARDSHIP OF GOD'S GIFTS

Based on the gift they have received,
everyone should use it to serve others,
as good managers of the varied grace of God.
1 Peter 4:10 HCSB

The gifts that you possess are gifts from the Giver of all things good. Do you have a spiritual gift? Share it. Do you have a testimony about the things that Christ has done for you? Don't leave your story untold. Do you possess financial resources? Share them. Do you have particular talents? Hone your skills and use them for God's glory.

When you hoard the treasures that God has given you, you live in rebellion against His commandments. But, when you obey God by sharing His gifts freely and without fanfare, you invite Him to bless you more and more. Today, be a faithful steward of your talents and treasures. And then prepare yourself for even greater blessings that are sure to come.

The Lord has abundantly blessed me all of my life. I'm not trying to pay Him back for all of His wonderful gifts; I just realize that He gave them to me to give away.

Lisa Whelchel

When God crowns our merits, he is crowning nothing other than his gifts.

St. Augustine

If I find in myself a desire which no experience in this world can satisfy, the most probable explanation is that I was made for another world.

C. S. Lewis

TODAY'S PRAYER

Dear Lord, let me use my gifts, and let me help my friends and family discover theirs. Your gifts are priceless and eternal. May we, Your children, use them to the glory of Your kingdom, today and forever. Amen

WHAT KIND OF EXAMPLE?

*Be an example to the believers in word,
in conduct, in love, in spirit, in faith, in purity.*
1 Timothy 4:12 NKJV

What kind of example are you? Are you the kind of woman whose life serves as a genuine example of righteousness? Are you a woman whose behavior serves as a positive role model for young people? Are you the kind of woman whose actions, day in and day out, are based upon kindness, faithfulness, and a love for the Lord? If so, you are not only blessed by God, but you are also a powerful force for good in a world that desperately needs positive influences such as yours.

Corrie ten Boom advised, "Don't worry about what you do not understand. Worry about what you do understand in the Bible but do not live by." And that's sound advice because our families and friends are watching and so is God.

Your light is the truth of the Gospel message itself as well as your witness as to Who Jesus is and what He has done for you. Don't hide it.

Anne Graham Lotz

Our trustworthiness implies His trustworthiness.

Beth Moore

There is nothing anybody else can do that can stop God from using us . . . We can turn everything into a testimony.

Corrie ten Boom

In serving we uncover the greatest fulfillment within and become a stellar example of a woman who knows and loves Jesus.

Vonette Bright

TODAY'S PRAYER

Dear Lord, help me be a worthy example to my friends and to my family. Let the things that I say and the things that I do show everyone what it means to be a follower of Your Son. Amen

DAY 41

BIG DREAMS

With God's power working in us,
God can do much, much more than anything
we can ask or imagine.
Ephesians 3:20 NCV

A re you willing to entertain the possibility that God has big plans in store for you? Hopefully so. Yet sometimes, especially if you've recently experienced a life-altering disappointment, you may find it difficult to envision a brighter future for yourself and your family. If so, it's time to reconsider your own capabilities . . . and God's.

God created you with unique gifts and untapped talents; your job is to tap them. When you do, you'll begin to feel an increasing sense of confidence in yourself and in your future.

It takes courage to dream big dreams. You will discover that courage when you do three things: accept the past, trust God to handle the future, and make the most of the time He has given you.

Sometimes our dreams were so big that it took two people to dream them.

Marie T. Freeman

Always stay connected to people and seek out things that bring you joy. Dream with abandon. Pray confidently.

Barbara Johnson

If all things are possible with God, then all things are possible to him who believes in him.

Corrie ten Boom

TODAY'S PRAYER

Dear Lord, give me the courage to dream and the faithfulness to trust in Your perfect plan. When I am worried or weary, give me strength for today and hope for tomorrow. Keep me mindful of Your healing power, Your infinite love, and Your eternal salvation. Amen

DAY 42

GET INVOLVED
IN A CHURCH

For where two or three are gathered together in
My name, I am there among them.
Matthew 18:20 HCSB

I f you want to build character, the church is
a wonderful place to do it. Are you an active, contributing, member of your local fellowship? The answer to this simple question will
have a profound impact on the direction of your
spiritual journey and the content of your character.

So do yourself a favor: Find a congregation
you're comfortable with, and join it. And once
you've joined, don't just attend church out of
habit. Go to church out of a sincere desire to
know and worship God. When you do, you'll be
blessed by the men and women who attend your
fellowship, and you'll be blessed by your Creator.
You deserve to attend church, and God deserves
for you to attend church, so don't delay.

Our churches are meant to be havens where the caste rules of the world do not apply.

Beth Moore

Be filled with the Holy Spirit; join a church where the members believe the Bible and know the Lord; seek the fellowship of other Christians; learn and be nourished by God's Word and His many promises. Conversion is not the end of your journey—it is only the beginning.

Corrie ten Boom

Someone has said that the Church at its very worst is better than the world at its best.

Gloria Gaither

TODAY'S PRAYER

Dear Lord, today I pray for Your church. Let me help to feed Your flock by helping to build Your church so that others, too, might experience Your enduring love and Your eternal grace. Amen

DAY 43

OPEN UP YOUR HEART

*We know that all things work together for
the good of those who love God: those who are
called according to His purpose.*
Romans 8:28 HCSB

C. S. Lewis observed, "A man's spiritual
health is exactly proportional to his love
for God." If we are to enjoy the spiritual
health that God intends for us, we must praise
Him, we must love Him, and we must obey Him.

When we worship God faithfully and obedi-
ently, we invite His love into our hearts. When
we truly worship God, we allow Him to rule
over our days and our lives. In turn, we grow to
love God even more deeply as we sense His love
for us.

Today, open your heart to the Father. And let
your obedience be a fitting response to His never-
ending love.

Joy is a by-product not of happy circumstances, education or talent, but of a healthy relationship with God and a determination to love Him no matter what.

Barbara Johnson

Delighting thyself in the Lord is the sudden realization that He has become the desire of your heart.

Beth Moore

Loving Him means the thankful acceptance of all things that His love has appointed.

Elisabeth Elliot

TODAY'S PRAYER

Dear Heavenly Father, You have blessed me with a love that is infinite and eternal. Let me love You, Lord, more and more each day. Make me a loving servant, Father, today and throughout eternity. And, let me show my love for You by sharing Your message and Your love with others. Amen

KNOWING GOD'S BOOK

Like newborn infants,
desire the unadulterated spiritual milk,
so that you may grow by it in your salvation.
1 Peter 2:2 HCSB

As a spiritual being, you have the potential to grow in your personal knowledge of the Lord every day that you live. You can do so through prayer, through worship, through an openness to God's Holy Spirit, and through a careful study of God's Holy Word.

Your Bible contains powerful prescriptions for everyday living. If you sincerely seek to walk with God, you should commit yourself to the thoughtful study of His teachings. The Bible can and should be your roadmap for every aspect of your life.

Do you seek to establish a closer relationship with your Heavenly Father? Then study His Word every day, with no exceptions. The Holy Bible is a priceless, one-of-a-kind gift from God. Treat it that way and read it that way.

Don't worry about what you do not understand of the Bible. Worry about what you do understand and do not live by.

Corrie ten Boom

The key to my understanding of the Bible is a personal relationship to Jesus Christ.

Oswald Chambers

If you believe what you like in the Gospel and reject what you don't like, it is not the Gospel you believe, but yourself.

St. Augustine

TODAY'S PRAYER

Heavenly Father, Your Holy Word is a light unto my path. In all that I do, help me be a worthy witness for You as I share the Good News of Your perfect Son and Your perfect Word. Amen

DAY 45

LET GOD JUDGE

Do not judge, and you will not be judged.
Do not condemn, and you will not be condemned.
Forgive, and you will be forgiven.

Luke 6:37 HCSB

We have all fallen short of God's commandments, and He has forgiven us. We, too, must forgive others. And, we must refrain from judging them.

Are you one of those people who finds it easy to judge others? If so, it's time to change.

God does not need (or, for that matter, want) your help. Why? Because God is perfectly capable of judging the human heart . . . while you are not.

As Christians, we are warned that to judge others is to invite fearful consequences: to the extent we judge others, so, too, will we be judged by God. Let us refrain, then, from judging our neighbors. Instead, let us forgive them and love them in the same way that God has forgiven us.

Christians think they are prosecuting attorneys or judges, when, in reality, God has called all of us to be witnesses.

Warren Wiersbe

On judgment day you'll meet Father God—not Mother Earth!

Anonymous

No creed or school of thought can monopolize the Spirit of God.

Oswald Chambers

TODAY'S PRAYER

Dear Lord, sometimes I am quick to judge others. But, You have commanded me not to judge. Keep me mindful, Father, that when I judge others, I am living outside of Your will for my life. You have forgiven me, Lord. Let me forgive others, let me love them, and let me help them . . . without judging them. Amen

DAY 46

ASK HIM FOR THE THINGS YOU NEED

You do not have because you do not ask.

James 4:2 HCSB

God gives the gifts; we, as believers, should accept them—but oftentimes, we don't. Why? Because we fail to trust our Heavenly Father completely, and because we are, at times, surprisingly stubborn. Luke 11 teaches us that God does not withhold spiritual gifts from those who ask. Our obligation, quite simply, is to ask for them.

Are you a woman who asks God to move mountains in your life, or are you expecting Him to stumble over molehills? Whatever the size of your challenges, God is big enough to handle them. Ask for His help today, with faith and with fervor, and then watch in amazement as your mountains begin to move.

God will help us become the people we are meant to be, if only we will ask Him.

Hannah Whitall Smith

When trials come your way—as inevitably they will—do not run away. Run to your God and Father.

Kay Arthur

By asking in Jesus' name, we're making a request not only in His authority, but also for His interests and His benefit.

Shirley Dobson

TODAY'S PRAYER

Dear Lord, today I will ask You for the things I need. In every circumstance, in every season of life, I will come to You in prayer. You know the desires of my heart, Lord; grant them, I ask. Yet not my will, Father, but Your will be done. Amen

DAY 47

YOU AND YOUR FAMILY

But if any widow has children or grandchildren,
they should learn to practice their religion
toward their own family first and to repay
their parents, for this pleases God.

1 Timothy 5:4 HCSB

As every woman knows, family life is a mixture of conversations, mediations, irritations, deliberations, frustrations, negotiations and celebrations. In other words, the life of the typical woman is incredibly varied. For those who are lucky enough to live in the presence of a close-knit, caring clan, the rewards far outweigh the frustrations. That's why we pray fervently for our family members, and that's why we love them despite their faults.

No family is perfect, and neither is yours. But, despite the inevitable challenges and occasional hurt feelings of family life, your clan is God's gift to you. They are a priceless treasure on temporary loan from the Father above. Give thanks to God for the gift of family . . . and act accordingly.

One way or the other, God, who thought up the family in the first place, has the very best idea of how to bring sense to the chaos of broken relationships we see all around us. I really believe that if I remain still and listen a lot, He will share some solutions with me so I can share them with others.

Jill Briscoe

When God asks someone to do something for Him entailing sacrifice, he makes up for it in surprising ways. Though He has led Bill all over the world to preach the gospel, He has not forgotten the little family in the mountains of North Carolina.

Ruth Bell Graham

TODAY'S PRAYER

Dear Lord, I am part of Your family, and I praise You for Your gift of my earthly family. I pray for them, that they might be protected and blessed by You. Let me show love and acceptance for my family, Lord, so that through me, they might come to know and to love You. Amen

DAY 48

BE STILL

Be still, and know that I am God.
Psalm 46:10 NKJV

In the first chapter of Mark, we read that in the darkness of the early morning hours, Jesus went to a solitary place and prayed. So, too, should we. But sometimes, finding quiet moments of solitude is difficult indeed.

We live in a noisy world, a world filled with distractions, frustrations, and complications. But if we allow the distractions of a clamorous world to separate us from God's peace, we do ourselves a profound disservice.

Has the busy pace of life robbed you of the peace that might otherwise be yours through Jesus Christ? Nothing is more important than the time you spend with your Savior. So be still and claim the inner peace that is your spiritual birthright: the peace of Jesus Christ. It is offered freely; it has been paid for in full; it is yours for the asking. So ask. And then share.

The manifold rewards of a serious, consistent prayer life demonstrate clearly that time with our Lord should be our first priority.

Shirley Dobson

The Lord Jesus, available to people much of the time, left them, sometimes a great while before day, to go up to the hills where He could commune in solitude with His Father.

Elisabeth Elliot

Jesus taught us by example to get out of the rat race and recharge our batteries.

Barbara Johnson

TODAY'S PRAYER

Lord, Your Holy Word is a light unto the world; let me study it, trust it, and share it with all who cross my path. Let me discover You, Father, in the quiet moments of the day. And, in all that I say and do, help me to be a worthy witness as I share the Good News of Your perfect Son and Your perfect Word. Amen

DAY 49

YOUR BRIGHT FUTURE

*"For I know the plans I have for you"—[this is]
the Lord's declaration—"plans for [your] welfare,
not for disaster, to give you a future and a hope."*
Jeremiah 29:11 HCSB

How bright is your future? Well, if you're a faithful believer, God's plans for you are so bright that you'd better wear shades. But here's an important question: How bright do you believe your future to be? Are you expecting a terrific tomorrow, or are you dreading a terrible one? The answer you give will have a powerful impact on the way tomorrow turns out.

Do you trust in the ultimate goodness of God's plan for your life? Will you face tomorrow's challenges with optimism and hope? You should. After all, God created you for a very important reason: His reason. And you still have important work to do: His work.

Today, as you live in the present and look to the future, remember that God has an amazing plan for you. Act—and believe—accordingly.

You can look forward with hope, because one day there will be no more separation, no more scars, and no more suffering in My Father's House. It's the home of your dreams!

Anne Graham Lotz

The best we can hope for in this life is a knothole peek at the shining realities ahead. Yet a glimpse is enough. It's enough to convince our hearts that whatever sufferings and sorrows currently assail us aren't worthy of comparison to that which waits over the horizon.

Joni Eareckson Tada

TODAY'S PRAYER

Dear Lord, as I look to the future, I will place my trust in You. If I become discouraged, I will turn to You. If I am afraid, I will seek strength in You. You are my Father, and I will place my hope, my trust, and my faith in You. Amen

DAY 50

PAYING ATTENTION TO GOD

For where your treasure is,
there your heart will be also.
Luke 12:34 HCSB

Who is in charge of your heart? Is it God, or is it something else? Have you given Christ your heart, your soul, your talents, your time, and your testimony? Or are you giving Him little more than a few hours each Sunday morning?

In the book of Exodus, God warns that we should place no gods before Him. Yet all too often, we place our Lord in second, third, or fourth place as we worship other things. When we unwittingly place possessions or relationships above our love for the Creator, we create big problems for ourselves.

Does God rule your heart? Make certain that the honest answer to this question is a resounding yes. In the life of every radical believer, God comes first.

He is always thinking about us. We are before his eyes. The Lord's eye never sleeps, but is always watching out for our welfare. We are continually on his heart.

C. H. Spurgeon

God loves each of us as if there were only one of us.

St. Augustine

Even before God created the heavens and the earth, He knew you and me, and He chose us! You and I were born because it was God's good pleasure.

Kay Arthur

TODAY'S PRAYER

Your faithfulness, Lord, is everlasting. You are faithful to me even when I am not faithful to You. Today, let me serve You with my heart, my soul, and my mind. And, then, let me rest in the knowledge of Your unchanging and constant love for me. Amen

BE CAREFUL HOW YOU DIRECT YOUR THOUGHTS

Blessed are the pure in heart, because they will see God.
Matthew 5:8 HCSB

Thoughts are intensely powerful things. Our thoughts have the power to lift us up or drag us down; they have the power to energize us or deplete us, to inspire us to greater accomplishments, or to make those accomplishments impossible.

If negative thoughts have left you worried, exhausted, or both, it's time to readjust your thought patterns. Negative thinking is habit-forming; thankfully, so is positive thinking. And it's up to you to train your mind to focus on God's power and your possibilities. Both are far greater than you can imagine.

As we have by faith said no to sin, so we should by faith say yes to God and set our minds on things above, where Christ is seated in the heavenlies.

Vonette Bright

Attitude is the mind's paintbrush; it can color any situation.

Barbara Johnson

The things we think are the things that feed our souls. If we think on pure and lovely things, we shall grow pure and lovely like them; and the converse is equally true.

Hannah Whitall Smith

TODAY'S PRAYER

Dear Lord, I will focus on Your love, Your power, Your promises, and Your Son. When I am weak, I will turn to You for strength; when I am worried, I will turn to You for comfort; when I am troubled, I will turn to You for patience and perspective. Help me guard my thoughts, Lord, so that I may honor You this day and forever. Amen

DAY 52

BE PATIENT AND
TRUST GOD

*Trust in Him at all times, you people; pour out your
heart before Him; God is a refuge for us.*

Psalm 62:8 NKJV

As busy women in a fast-paced world, many of us find that waiting quietly for God is difficult. Why? Because we are fallible human beings seeking to live according to our own timetables, not God's. In our better moments, we realize that patience is not only a virtue, but it is also a commandment from God.

We human beings are impatient by nature. We know what we want, and we know exactly when we want it: NOW! But, God knows better. He has created a world that unfolds according to His plans, not our own.

God instructs us to be patient in all things. We must be patient with our families, our friends, and our associates. We must also be patient with God as He unfolds His plan for our lives. After all, think how patient God has been with us.

Waiting is the hardest kind of work, but God knows best, and we may joyfully leave all in His hands.

Lottie Moon

Wisdom always waits for the right time to act, while emotion always pushes for action right now.

Joyce Meyer

How do you wait upon the Lord? First you must learn to sit at His feet and take time to listen to His words.

Kay Arthur

TODAY'S PRAYER

Lord, give me patience. When I am hurried, give me peace. When I am frustrated, give me perspective. When I am angry, let me turn my heart to You. Today, let me become a more patient woman, Dear Lord, as I trust in You and in Your master plan for my life. Amen

DAY 53

IF YOU REACH OUT TO GOD . . .

Draw near to God, and He will draw near to you.
James 4:8 HCSB

Do you ever wonder if God is really "right here, right now"? Do you wonder if God hears your prayers, if He understands your feelings, or if He really knows your heart? If so, you're not alone: lots of very faithful Christians have experienced periods of doubt. In fact, some of the biggest heroes in the Bible had plenty of doubts—and so, perhaps, will you. But when you have doubts, remember this: God isn't on a coffee break, and He hasn't moved out of town. God isn't taking a long vacation, and He isn't snoozing on the couch. He's right here, right now, listening to your thoughts and prayers, watching over your every move.

If you'd like to get to know God a little bit better, He's always available—always ready to listen to your prayers, and always ready to speak to your heart. Are you ready to talk to Him?

You cannot grow spiritually until you have the assurance that Christ is in your life.

Vonette Bright

Here is our opportunity: we cannot see God, but we can see Christ. Christ was not only the Son of God, but He was the Father. Whatever Christ was, that God is.

Hannah Whitall Smith

Christians have spent their whole lives mastering all sorts of principles, done their duty, carried on the programs of their church . . . and never known God intimately, heart to heart.

John Eldredge

Today's Prayer

Dear Lord, give me the wisdom to seek You, the patience to wait for You, the insight to hear You, and the courage to obey You, this day and forever. Amen

HOLINESS BEFORE HAPPINESS

Blessed are those who hunger and thirst for righteousness, because they will be filled.
Matthew 5:6 HCSB

How do we live a life that is "right with God"? By accepting God's Son and obeying His commandments. Accepting Christ is a decision that we make one time; following in His footsteps requires thousands of decisions each day.

Whose steps will you follow today? Will you honor God as you strive to follow His Son? Or will you join the lockstep legion that seeks to discover happiness and fulfillment through worldly means? If you are righteous and wise, you will follow Christ. You will follow Him today and every day. You will seek to walk in His footsteps without reservation or doubt. When you do so, you will be "right with God" precisely because you are walking aright with His only begotten Son.

Holiness has never been the driving force of the majority. It is, however, mandatory for anyone who wants to enter the kingdom.

Elisabeth Elliot

Our afflictions are designed not to break us but to bend us toward the eternal and the holy.

Barbara Johnson

One of the first things the Holy Spirit does when He comes into your life is to give you a desire to be holy.

Anne Graham Lotz

TODAY'S PRAYER

Lord, You are a righteous and Holy God, and You have called me to be a righteous woman. When I fall short, forgive me and renew a spirit of holiness within me. Lead me, Lord, along Your path, and guide me far from the temptations of this world. Let Your Holy Word guide my actions, and let Your love reside in my heart, this day and every day. Amen

HAVE THE COURAGE TO TRUST GOD

Trust in the Lord with all your heart, and do not rely on your own understanding; think about Him in all your ways, and He will guide you on the right paths.

Proverbs 3:5-6 HCSB

When our dreams come true and our plans prove successful, we find it easy to thank our Creator and easy to trust His divine providence. But in times of sorrow or hardship, we may find ourselves questioning God's plans for our lives.

Are you a woman who seeks God's blessings for yourself and your family? Then trust Him. Trust Him with your relationships. Trust Him with your priorities. Follow His commandments and pray for His guidance. Trust Your Heavenly Father day by day, moment by moment—in good times and in trying times. Then, wait patiently for God's revelations . . . and prepare yourself for the abundance and peace that will most certainly be yours when you do.

Do not be afraid, then, that if you trust, or tell others to trust, the matter will end there. Trust is only the beginning and the continual foundation. When we trust Him, the Lord works, and His work is the important part of the whole matter.

Hannah Whitall Smith

Are you serious about wanting God's guidance to become the person he wants you to be? The first step is to tell God that you know you can't manage your own life; that you need his help.

Catherine Marshall

Never be afraid to trust an unknown future to a known God.

Corrie ten Boom

TODAY'S PRAYER

Dear Lord, let my faith be in You, and in You alone. Without You, I am weak, but when I trust You, I am protected. In every aspect of my life, Father, let me place my hope and my trust in Your infinite wisdom and Your boundless grace. Amen

LET GOD GUIDE
THE WAY

*The true children of God are those who
let God's Spirit lead them.*
Romans 8:14 NCV

The Bible promises that God will guide you if you let Him. Your job, of course, is to let Him. But sometimes, you will be tempted to do otherwise. Sometimes, you'll be tempted to go along with the crowd; other times, you'll be tempted to do things your way, not God's way. When you feel those temptations, resist them.

What will you allow to guide you through the coming day: your own desires or will you allow God to lead the way? The answer should be obvious. You should let God be your guide. When you entrust your life to Him completely and without reservation, God will give you the strength to meet any challenge, the courage to face any trial, and the wisdom to live in His righteousness.

Are you serious about wanting God's guidance to become a personal reality in your life? The first step is to tell God that you know you can't manage your own life; that you need his help.

Catherine Marshall

We have ample evidence that the Lord is able to guide. The promises cover every imaginable situation. All we need to do is to take the hand he stretches out.

Elisabeth Elliot

God's guidance is even more important than common sense. I can declare that the deepest darkness is outshone by the light of Jesus.

Corrie ten Boom

TODAY'S PRAYER

Lord, You have a plan for my life. Let me discover it and live it. Today, I will seek Your will, knowing that when I trust in You, Dear Father, I am eternally blessed. Amen

PRAY FOR GOD'S ABUNDANCE

I have come that they may have life,
and that they may have it more abundantly.
John 10:10 NKJV

The familiar words of John 10:10 should serve as a daily reminder: Christ came to this earth so that we might experience His abundance, His love, and His gift of eternal life. But Christ does not force Himself upon us; we must claim His gifts for ourselves.

Every woman knows that some days are so busy and so hurried that abundance seems a distant promise. It is not. Every day, we can claim the spiritual abundance that God promises for our lives . . . and we should.

Hannah Whitall Smith observed, "God is the giver, and we are the receivers. And His richest gifts are bestowed not upon those who do the greatest things, but upon those who accept His abundance and His grace." Christ is, indeed, the Giver. Will you accept His gifts today?

The gift of God is eternal life, spiritual life, abundant life through faith in Jesus Christ, the Living Word of God.

Anne Graham Lotz

God's riches are beyond anything we could ask or even dare to imagine! If my life gets gooey and stale, I have no excuse.

Barbara Johnson

It would be wrong to have a "poverty complex," for to think ourselves paupers is to deny either the King's riches or to deny our being His children.

Catherine Marshall

TODAY'S PRAYER

Dear Lord, thank You for the joyful, abundant life that is mine through Christ Jesus. Guide me according to Your will, and help me become a woman whose life is a worthy example to others. Give me courage, Lord, to claim the spiritual riches that You have promised, and show me Your plan for my life, today and forever. Amen

DAY 58

TRUST GOD'S WISDOM

Insight is a fountain of life for its possessor,
but folly is the instruction of fools.

Proverbs 16:22 HCSB

Where will you place your trust today? Will you trust in the wisdom of fallible men and women, or will you place your faith in God's perfect wisdom? When you decide whom to trust, you will then know how best to respond to the challenges of the coming day.

Are you tired? Discouraged? Fearful? Be comforted and trust God. Are you worried or anxious? Be confident in God's power and trust His Holy Word. Are you confused? Listen to the quiet voice of your Heavenly Father. He is not a God of confusion. Talk with Him; listen to Him; trust Him. He is steadfast, and He is your Protector . . . forever.

If you are struggling to make some difficult decisions right now that aren't specifically addressed in the Bible, don't make a choice based on what's right for someone else. You are the Lord's and He will make sure you do what's right.

Lisa Whelchel

Make God's will the focus of your life day by day. If you seek to please Him and Him alone, you'll find yourself satisfied with life.

Kay Arthur

The will of God is never exactly what you expect it to be. It may seem to be much worse, but in the end it's going to be a lot better and a lot bigger.

Elisabeth Elliot

TODAY'S PRAYER

Dear Lord, You are my Teacher. Help me to learn from You. And then, let me show others what it means to be a kind, generous, loving Christian. Amen

DAY 59

SEE THROUGH
THE MEDIA'S
DISTORTED MESSAGES

*Do not love the world or the things that belong
to the world. If anyone loves the world,
love for the Father is not in him.*
1 John 2:15 HCSB

B eware! The media is working around the
clock in an attempt to rearrange your priorities. The media says that appearance is
all-important, that thinness is all-important, and
that social standing is all-important. But guess
what? Those messages are untrue. The important
things in life have little to do with appearances.
The all-important things in life have to do with
your faith, your family, and your future. Period.

Because you live in the 21st century, you are
relentlessly bombarded by media messages that
are contrary to your faith. Take those messages
with a grain of salt—or better yet, don't take
them at all.

Every Christian is a contradiction to this old world. He crosses it at every point. He goes against the grain from beginning to end. From the day that he is born again until the day that he goes on to be with the Lord, he must stand against the current of a world always going the other way.

Vance Havner

A fish would never be happy living on land, because it was made for water. An eagle could never feel satisfied if it wasn't allowed to fly. You will never feel completely satisfied on earth, because you were made for more.

Rick Warren

TODAY'S PRAYER

Lord, this world is filled with temptations and distractions; we have many opportunities to stray from Your commandments. Help us to focus not on the things of this world, but on the message of Your Son. Let us keep Christ in our hearts as we follow Him this day and forever. Amen

THE DECISION TO
CELEBRATE LIFE

*This is the day the Lord has made;
let us rejoice and be glad in it.*

Psalm 118:24 HCSB

The 100th Psalm reminds us that the entire earth should "Shout for joy to the Lord." As God's children, we are blessed beyond measure, but sometimes, as busy women living in a demanding world, we are slow to count our gifts and even slower to give thanks to the Giver.

Our blessings include life and health, family and friends, freedom and possessions—for starters. And, the gifts we receive from God are multiplied when we share them. May we always give thanks to God for His blessings, and may we always demonstrate our gratitude by sharing our gifts with others.

The 118th Psalm reminds us that, "This is the day which the LORD has made; let us rejoice and be glad in it" (v. 24, NASB). May we celebrate this day and the One who created it.

If you can forgive the person you were, accept the person you are, and believe in the person you will become, you are headed for joy. So celebrate your life.

Barbara Johnson

Christ is the secret, the source, the substance, the center, and the circumference of all true and lasting gladness.

Mrs. Charles E. Cowman

God knows everything. He can manage everything, and He loves us. Surely this is enough for a fullness of joy that is beyond words.

Hannah Whitall Smith

TODAY'S PRAYER

Dear Lord, help us remember that every day is cause for celebration. Today we will try our best to keep joy in our hearts. We will celebrate the life You have given us here on earth and the eternal life that will be ours in heaven. Amen

DAY 61

FOLLOW HIM

If anyone serves Me, let him follow Me;
and where I am, there My servant will be also.
If anyone serves Me, him My Father will honor.
John 12:26 NKJV

Jesus loved you so much that He endured unspeakable humiliation and suffering for you. How will you respond to Christ's sacrifice? Will you take up His cross and follow Him (Luke 9:23), or will you choose another path? When you place your hopes squarely at the foot of the cross, when you place Jesus squarely at the center of your life, you will be blessed. If you seek to be a worthy disciple of Jesus, you must acknowledge that He never comes "next." He is always first.

Do you hope to fulfill God's purpose for your life? Do you seek a life of abundance and peace? Do you intend to be Christian not just in name, but in deed? Then follow Christ. Follow Him by picking up His cross today and every day that you live. When you do, you will quickly discover that Christ's love has the power to change everything.

Peter said, "No, Lord!" But he had to learn that one cannot say "No" while saying "Lord" and that one cannot say "Lord" while saying "No."

Corrie ten Boom

You cannot cooperate with Jesus in becoming what He wants you to become and simultaneously be what the world desires to make you. If you would say, "Take the world but give me Jesus," then you must deny yourself and take up your cross. The simple truth is that your "self" must be put to death in order for you to get to the point where for you to live is Christ. What will it be? The world and you, or Jesus and you? You do have a choice to make.

Kay Arthur

TODAY'S PRAYER

Dear Jesus, because I am Your disciple, I will trust You, I will obey Your teachings, and I will share Your Good News. You have given me life abundant and life eternal, and I will follow You today and forever. Amen

CHOOSING TO BE KIND

*And may the Lord make you increase
and abound in love to one another and to all.*

1 Thessalonians 3:12 NKJV

Christ showed His love for us by willingly sacrificing His own life so that we might have eternal life: "But God demonstrates his own love for us in this: While we were still sinners, Christ died for us" (Romans 5:8 NIV). We, as Christ's followers, are challenged to share His love with kind words on our lips and praise in our hearts.

Just as Christ has been—and will always be—the ultimate friend to His flock, so should we be Christlike in the kindness and generosity that we show toward others, especially those who are most in need.

When we walk each day with Jesus—and obey the commandments found in God's Holy Word—we become worthy ambassadors for Christ. When we share the love of Christ, we share a priceless gift with the world.

Kindness in this world will do much to help others, not only to come into the light, but also to grow in grace day by day.

Fanny Crosby

All kindness and good deeds, we must keep silent. The result will be an inner reservoir of personality power.

Catherine Marshall

The attitude of kindness is everyday stuff like a great pair of sneakers. Not frilly. Not fancy. Just plain and comfortable.

Barbara Johnson

TODAY'S PRAYER

Lord, sometimes this world can become a place of busyness, frustration, and confusion. Slow me down, Lord, that I might see the needs of those around me. And every day, Lord, let my love for Christ be reflected through deeds of kindness for those who need the healing touch of the Master's hand. Amen

DAY 63

TOO BUSY?

Be careful not to forget the Lord.
Deuteronomy 6:12 HCSB

Has the busy pace of life robbed you of the peace that might otherwise be yours through Jesus Christ? If so, you are simply too busy for your own good. Through His Son Jesus, God offers you a peace that passes human understanding, but He won't force His peace upon you; in order to experience it, you must slow down long enough to sense His presence and His love.

Today, as a gift to yourself, to your family, and to the world, slow down and claim the inner peace that is your spiritual birthright: the peace of Jesus Christ. It is offered freely; it has been paid for in full; it is yours for the asking. So ask. And then share.

In our tense, uptight society where folks are rushing to make appointments they have already missed, a good laugh can be a refreshing as a cup of cold water in the desert.

Barbara Johnson

Frustration is not the will of God. There is time to do anything and everything that God wants us to do.

Elisabeth Elliot

God is more concerned with the direction of your life than with its speed.

Marie T. Freeman

TODAY'S PRAYER

Dear Lord, when the quickening pace of life leaves me with little time for worship or for praise, help me to reorder my priorities. When the demands of the day leave me distracted and discouraged, let me turn to Jesus for the peace that only He can give. Amen

DAY 64

BE AWARE OF
YOUR BLESSINGS

*Therefore, get your minds ready for action,
being self-disciplined, and set your hope completely
on the grace to be brought to you
at the revelation of Jesus Christ.*
1 Peter 1:13 HCSB

Psalm 145 makes this promise: "The LORD is gracious and compassionate, slow to anger and rich in love. The LORD is good to all; he has compassion on all he has made" (vv. 8-9 NIV). As God's children, we are blessed beyond measure, but sometimes, as busy women in a demanding world, we are slow to count our gifts and even slower to give thanks to the Giver. Our blessings include life and health, family and friends, freedom and possessions—for starters. And, the gifts we receive from God are multiplied when we share them with others. May we always give thanks to God for our blessings, and may we always demonstrate our gratitude by sharing them.

Do we not continually pass by blessings innumerable without notice, and instead fix our eyes on what we feel to be our trials and our losses, and think and talk about these until our whole horizon is filled with them, and we almost begin to think we have no blessings at all?

Hannah Whitall Smith

When you and I are related to Jesus Christ, our strength and wisdom and peace and joy and love and hope may run out, but His life rushes in to keep us filled to the brim. We are showered with blessings, not because of anything we have or have not done, but simply because of Him.

Anne Graham Lotz

TODAY'S PRAYER

Lord, let me be a woman who counts her blessings, and let me be Your faithful servant as I give praise to the Giver of all things good. You have richly blessed my life, Lord. Let me, in turn, be a blessing to all those who cross my path, and may the glory be Yours forever. Amen

HIS DISCIPLE

*He has told you men what is good and what it is
the Lord requires of you: Only to act justly,
to love faithfulness, and to walk humbly
with your God.*

Micah 6:8 HCSB

When Jesus addressed His disciples, He warned that each one must "take up his cross and follow me." The disciples must have known exactly what the Master meant. In Jesus' day, prisoners were forced to carry their own crosses to the location where they would be put to death. Thus, Christ's message was clear: in order to follow Him, Christ's disciples must deny themselves and, instead, trust Him completely. Nothing has changed since then.

Do you seek to be a worthy disciple of Christ? Then pick up His cross today and every day that you live. When you do, He will bless you now and forever.

Jesus challenges you and me to keep our focus daily on the cross of His will if we want to be His disciples.

Anne Graham Lotz

When Jesus put the little child in the midst of His disciples, He did not tell the little child to become like His disciples; He told the disciples to become like the little child.

Ruth Bell Graham

TODAY'S PRAYER

Dear Lord, thank You for the gift of Your Son Jesus, my personal Savior. Let me be a worthy disciple of Christ, and let me be ever grateful for His love. I offer my life to You, Lord, so that I might live according to Your commandments and according to Your plan. I will praise You always as I give thanks for Your Son and for Your everlasting love. Amen

CHOOSING TO BEHAVE DIFFERENTLY

As God's slaves, live as free people,
but don't use your freedom as a way to conceal evil.
1 Peter 2:16 HCSB

Life is a series of choices. Each day, we make countless decisions that can bring us closer to God . . . or not. When we live according to God's commandments, we earn for ourselves the abundance and peace that He intends for our lives. But, when we turn our backs upon God by ignoring Him—or by disobeying Him—we bring needless pain and suffering upon ourselves and our families.

When you're faced with a difficult choice or a powerful temptation, seek God's counsel and trust the counsel He gives. Invite God into your heart and live according to His commandments. And when God speaks to you through that little quiet voice that He has placed in your heart, listen. When you do, you will be blessed today, and tomorrow, and forever.

We have a decision to make—to turn away from sin or to be miserable and suffer the consequences of continual disobedience.

Vonette Bright

When your good behavior speaks for itself . . . don't interrupt.

Anonymous

Although God causes all things to work together for good for His children, He still holds us accountable for our behavior.

Kay Arthur

TODAY'S PRAYER

Dear Lord, this world has countless temptations, distractions, interruptions, and frustrations. When I allow my focus to drift away from You and Your Word, I suffer. But, when I turn my thoughts and my prayers to You, Heavenly Father, You guide my path. Let me discover the right thing to do—and let me do it—this day and every day that I live. Amen

DAY 67

CRITICS BEWARE

Don't criticize one another, brothers. He who criticizes
a brother or judges his brother criticizes the law
and judges the law. But if you judge the law,
you are not a doer of the law but a judge.

James 4:11 HCSB

From experience, we know that it is easier to criticize than to correct; we understand that it is easier to find faults than solutions; and we realize that excessive criticism is usually destructive, not productive. Yet the urge to criticize others remains a powerful temptation for most of us.

Negativity is highly contagious: we give it to others who, in turn, give it back to us. This cycle can be broken by positive thoughts, heartfelt prayers, and encouraging words. As thoughtful servants of a loving God, we can use the transforming power of Christ's love to break the chains of negativity. And we should.

Being critical of others, including God, is one way we try to avoid facing and judging our own sins.

Warren Wiersbe

The scrutiny we give other people should be for ourselves.

Oswald Chambers

After one hour in heaven, we shall be ashamed that we ever grumbled.

Vance Havner

A pessimist is someone who believes that when her cup runneth over she'll need a mop.

Barbara Johnson

TODAY'S PRAYER

Help me, Lord, rise above the need to criticize others. May my own shortcomings humble me, and may I always be a source of genuine encouragement to my family and friends. Amen

FOCUS ON
THE RIGHT STUFF

Let your eyes look forward;
fix your gaze straight ahead.
Proverbs 4:25 HCSB

This day—and every day hereafter—is a chance to celebrate the life that God has given you. It's also a chance to give thanks to the One who has offered you more blessings than you can possibly count. What is your focus today? Are you willing to focus your thoughts and energies on God's blessings and upon His will for your life? Or will you turn your thoughts to other things?

Today, why not focus your thoughts on the joy that is rightfully yours in Christ? Why not take time to celebrate God's glorious creation? Why not trust your hopes instead of your fears? When you do, you will think optimistically about yourself and your world . . . and you can then share your optimism with others. They'll be better for it, and so will you.

We need to stop focusing on our lacks and stop giving out excuses and start looking at and listening to Jesus.

Anne Graham Lotz

Paul did one thing. Most of us dabble in forty things. Are you a doer or a dabbler?

Vance Havner

When Jesus is in our midst, He brings His limitless power along as well. But, Jesus must be in the middle, all eyes and hearts focused on Him.

Shirley Dobson

TODAY'S PRAYER

Dear Lord, help me to face this day with a spirit of optimism and thanksgiving. And let me focus my thoughts on You and Your incomparable gifts. Amen

YOU CAN ALWAYS ESCAPE TEMPTATION

*The Lord knows how to deliver
the godly out of temptations.*
2 Peter 2:9 NKJV

I f you stop to think about it, the cold, hard evidence is right in front of your eyes: you live in a temptation-filled world. The devil is out on the street, hard at work, causing pain and heartache in more ways than ever before. Here in the 21st century, the bad guys are working around the clock to lead you astray.

In a letter to believers, Peter offered a stern warning: "Your adversary, the devil, prowls around like a roaring lion, seeking someone to devour" (1 Peter 5:8 NASB). What was true then is equally true now. Satan tempts his prey and then devours them. As believing Christians, we must beware. And, if we seek righteousness in our own lives, we must earnestly wrap ourselves in the protection of God's Holy Word. When we do, we are secure.

Because Christ has faced our every temptation without sin, we never face a temptation that has no door of escape.

Beth Moore

Lord, what joy to know that Your powers are so much greater than those of the enemy.

Corrie ten Boom

We, as God's people, are not only to stay far away from sin and sinners who would entice us, but we are to be so like our God that we mourn over sin.

Kay Arthur

TODAY'S PRAYER

Lord, life is filled with temptations to stray from Your chosen path. Keep me mindful that the life I live and the words I speak bear testimony to my faith. Make me a faithful servant of Your Son, and lead me far from the temptations of this world. Make me a righteous woman, Lord, and let my actions point others to You. Amen

LOVE ACCORDING
TO GOD

This is My commandment,
that you love one another as I have loved you.
John 15:12 NKJV

As a woman, you know the profound love that you hold in your heart for your own family and friends. As a child of God, you can only imagine the infinite love that your Heavenly Father holds for you.

God made you in His own image and gave you salvation through the person of His Son Jesus Christ. And now, precisely because you are a wondrous creation treasured by God, a question presents itself: What will you do in response to the Creator's love? Will you ignore it or embrace it? Will you return it or neglect it? That decision, of course, is yours and yours alone.

When you embrace God's love, your life's purpose is forever changed. God and His infinite love and mercy is waiting to embrace you with open arms. Accept His love today and forever.

It is when we come to the Lord in our nothing-ness, our powerlessness and our helplessness that He then enables us to love in a way which, without Him, would be absolutely impossible.

Elisabeth Elliot

Live your lives in love, the same sort of love which Christ gives us, and which He perfectly expressed when He gave Himself as a sacrifice to God.

Corrie ten Boom

To have fallen in love hints to our hearts that all of earthly life is not hopelessly fallen. Love is the laughter of God.

Beth Moore

TODAY'S PRAYER

Dear Lord, You have given me the gift of love; let me share that gift with others. And, keep me mindful that the essence of love is not to receive it, but to give it, today and forever. Amen

CHOICES

*But seek first the kingdom of God
and His righteousness, and all these things
will be provided for you.*
Matthew 6:33 HCSB

L ife is a series of decisions and choices. Each day, we make countless decisions that can bring us closer to God . . . or not. When we live according to God's commandments, we earn for ourselves the abundance and peace that He intends for our lives. But, when we turn our backs upon God by disobeying Him, we bring needless suffering upon ourselves and our families.

Do you seek spiritual abundance that can be yours through the person of God's only begotten Son? Then invite Christ into your heart and live according to His teachings. And, when you confront a difficult decision or a powerful temptation, seek God's wisdom and trust it. When you do, you will receive untold blessings—not only for this day, but also for all eternity.

Freedom is not the right to do what we want but the power to do what we ought.

Corrie ten Boom

I could go through this day oblivious to the miracles all around me or I could tune in and "enjoy."

Gloria Gaither

I do not know how the Spirit of Christ performs it, but He brings us choices through which we constantly change, fresh and new, into His likeness.

Joni Eareckson Tada

Every day of our lives we make choices about how we're going to live that day.

Luci Swindoll

TODAY'S PRAYER

Heavenly Father, I have many choices to make. Help me choose wisely as I follow in the footsteps of Your only begotten Son. Amen

LOOK FOR FULFILLMENT

I am the door. If anyone enters by Me,
he will be saved,
and will come in and go out and find pasture.
John 10:9 HCSB

Where can you find contentment? Is it a result of wealth, or power, or beauty, or fame? Hardly. Genuine contentment springs from a peaceful spirit, a clear conscience, and a loving heart (like yours!).

Our world seems preoccupied with the search for happiness. We are bombarded with messages telling us that happiness depends upon the acquisition of material possessions. These messages are false. Enduring peace is not the result of our acquisitions; it is the inevitable result of our dispositions. If we don't find contentment within ourselves, we will never find it outside ourselves.

Thus the search for contentment is an internal quest, an exploration of the heart, mind, and soul. You can find contentment—indeed you will find it—if you simply look in the right places.

Father and Mother lived on the edge of poverty, and yet their contentment was not dependent upon their surroundings. Their relationship to each other and to the Lord gave them strength and happiness.

Corrie ten Boom

Yes, we were created for His holy pleasure, but we will ultimately—if not immediately—find much pleasure in His pleasure.

Beth Moore

TODAY'S PRAYER

Father, let me be a woman who strives to do Your will, and as I do, let me find contentment and balance. Let me live in the light of Your will and Your priorities for my life, and when I have done my best, Lord, give me the wisdom to place my faith and my trust in You. Amen

DAY 73

PROBLEM-SOLVING 101

*People who do what is right may have
many problems, but the Lord will solve them all.*
Psalm 34:19 NCV

Face facts: the upcoming day will not be problem-free. In fact, your life can be viewed as an exercise in problem-solving. The question is not whether you will encounter problems; the real question is how you will choose to address them.

When it comes to solving the problems of everyday living, we often know precisely what needs to be done, but we may be slow in doing it—especially if what needs to be done is difficult or uncomfortable. So we put off till tomorrow what should be done today.

The words of Psalm 34 remind us that the Lord solves problems for "people who do what is right" (v. 19 NCV). Usually, doing "what is right" means doing the uncomfortable work of confronting our problems sooner rather than later.

He that is mastered by Christ is the master of every circumstance. Does the circumstance press hard against you? Do not push it away. It is the Potter's hand.

Mrs. Charles E. Cowman

When you are in deep water—trust the One who walked on it.

Anonymous

God had one son on earth without sin, but never one without suffering.

St. Augustine

TODAY'S PRAYER

Dear Heavenly Father, when I am troubled, You heal me. When I am afraid, You protect me. When I am discouraged, You lift me up. You are my unending source of strength, Lord; let me turn to You when I am weak. In times of adversity, let me trust Your plan and Your will for my life. And whatever my circumstances, Lord, let me always give the thanks and the glory to You. Amen

DAY 74

BE A CHEERFUL
CHRISTIAN

A cheerful heart has a continual feast.

Proverbs 15:15 HCSB

On some days, as every woman knows, it's hard to be cheerful. Sometimes, as the demands of the world increase and our energy sags, we feel less like "cheering up" and more like "tearing up." But even in our darkest hours, we can turn to God, and He will give us comfort.

Few things in life are more sad, or, for that matter, more absurd, than a grumpy Christian. Christ promises us lives of abundance and joy, but He does not force His joy upon us. We must claim His joy for ourselves, and when we do, Jesus, in turn, fills our spirits with His power and His love.

How can we receive from Christ the joy that is rightfully ours? By giving Him what is rightfully His: our hearts and our souls.

When we bring sunshine into the lives of others, we're warmed by it ourselves. When we spill a little happiness, it splashes on us.

Barbara Johnson

God is good, and heaven is forever. And if those two facts don't cheer you up, nothing will.

Marie T. Freeman

Be assured, my dear friend, that it is no joy to God in seeing you with a dreary countenance.

C. H. Spurgeon

TODAY'S PRAYER

Dear Lord, You have given me so many reasons to celebrate. Today, let me choose an attitude of cheerfulness. Let me be a joyful Christian, Lord, quick to smile and slow to anger. Let me share Your goodness with all whom I meet so that Your love might shine in me and through me. Amen

ANSWERING THE CALL

*I urge you now to live the life
to which God called you.*
Ephesians 4:1 NKJV

God is calling you to follow a specific path that He has chosen for your life. And it is vitally important that you heed that call. Otherwise, your talents and opportunities may go unused.

Have you already heard God's call? And are you pursuing it with vigor? If so, you're both fortunate and wise. But if you have not yet discovered what God intends for you to do with your life, keep searching and keep praying until you discover why the Creator put you here.

God has important work for you to do—work that no one else on earth can accomplish but you. God has placed you in a particular location, amid particular people, with unique opportunities to serve. And He has given you all the tools you need to succeed.

He treats us as sons, and all he asks in return is that we shall treat Him as a Father whom we can trust without anxiety. We must take the son's place of dependence and trust, and we must let Him keep the father's place of care and responsibility.

Hannah Whitall Smith

How much of our lives are, well, so daily. How often our hours are filled with the mundane, seemingly unimportant things that have to be done, whether at home or work. These very "daily" tasks could become a celebration of praise. "It is through consecration," someone has said, "that drudgery is made divine."

Gigi Graham Tchividjian

TODAY'S PRAYER

Father, You have called me, and I acknowledge that calling. I will study Your Word and seek Your guidance. Give me the wisdom to know Your will for my life and the courage to follow wherever You may lead me, today and forever. Amen

PRAY ABOUT
YOUR DECISIONS

*Now if any of you lacks wisdom, he should ask
God, who gives to all generously and without
criticizing, and it will be given to him. But let him
ask in faith without doubting. For the doubter is like
the surging sea, driven and tossed by the wind.*

James 1:5-6 HCSB

Have you fervently asked God for His guidance in every aspect of your life? Jesus made it clear to His disciples: they should pray always. So should we. Genuine, heartfelt prayer produces powerful changes in us and in our world. When we lift our hearts to our Father in heaven, we open ourselves to a never-ending source of divine wisdom and infinite love.

Do you sincerely seek to know God's purpose for your life? Then ask Him for direction—and keep asking Him every day. Whatever your need, no matter how great or small, pray about it and never lose hope. God is not just near; He is here, and He's ready to talk with you. Now!

Are you weak? Weary? Confused? Troubled? Pressured? How is your relationship with God? Is it held in its place of priority? I believe the greater the pressure, the greater your need for time alone with Him.

Kay Arthur

Prayer is the same as the breathing of air for the lungs. Exhaling makes us get rid of our dirty air. Inhaling gives clean air. To exhale is to confess, to inhale is to be filled with the Holy Spirit.

Corrie ten Boom

TODAY'S PRAYER

Dear Lord, I will be a woman of prayer. I will pray about matters great and small. I will bring my concerns to You, Father. I will listen for Your voice, and I will follow in the footsteps of Your Son. Amen

HE'S RIGHT HERE, RIGHT NOW

The Lord is with you when you are with Him.
If you seek Him, He will be found by you.
2 Chronicles 15:2 HCSB

Since God is everywhere, we are free to sense His presence whenever we take the time to quiet our souls and turn our prayers to Him. But sometimes, amid the incessant demands of everyday life, we turn our thoughts far from God; when we do, we suffer.

Do you set aside quiet moments each day to offer praise to your Creator? As a woman who has received the gift of God's grace, you most certainly should. Silence is a gift that you give to yourself and to God.

The familiar words of Psalm 46:10 remind us to "Be still, and know that I am God." When we do so, we encounter the awesome presence of our loving Father, and we are comforted in the knowledge that God is not just near. He is here.

It's a crazy world and life speeds by at a blur, yet God is right in the middle of the craziness. And anywhere, at anytime, we may turn to Him, hear His voice, feel His hand, and catch the fragrance of heaven.

Joni Eareckson Tada

Only a love that has no regard for vessels and jars—appearances or image—only a love that will lavish its most treasured essence on the feet of Jesus can produce the kind of fragrance that draws cynics and believers alike into His presence.

Gloria Gaither

TODAY'S PRAYER

Heavenly Father, help me to feel Your presence in every situation and every circumstance. You are with me, Lord, in times of celebration and in times of sorrow. You never leave my side even when it seems to me that You are far away. Today and every day, God, let me feel Your presence so that others might know You through me. Amen

DAY 78

WHEN MOUNTAINS NEED MOVING

I assure you: If anyone says to this mountain,
"Be lifted up and thrown into the sea,"
and does not doubt in his heart, but believes that
what he says will happen, it will be done for him.

Mark 11:23 HCSB

When a suffering woman sought healing by simply touching the hem of His garment, Jesus turned and said, "Daughter, be of good comfort; thy faith hath made thee whole" (Matthew 9:22 KJV). We, too, can be made whole when we place our faith completely and unwaveringly in the person of Jesus Christ.

If your faith is being tested to the point of breaking, know that your Savior is near. If you reach out to Him in faith, He will give you peace and heal your broken spirit. Be content to touch even the smallest fragment of the Master's garment, and He will make you whole.

Grace calls you to get up, throw off your blanket of helplessness, and to move on through life in faith.

Kay Arthur

Faith does not concern itself with the entire journey. One step is enough.

Mrs. Charles E. Cowman

When you and I place our faith in Jesus Christ and invite Him to come live within us, the Holy Spirit comes upon us, and the power of God overshadows us, and the life of Jesus is born within us.

Anne Graham Lotz

TODAY'S PRAYER

Dear Lord, help me to be a woman of faith. Help me to remember that You are always near and that You can overcome any challenge. With Your love and Your power, Lord, I can live courageously and faithfully today and every day. Amen

WORRY LESS

Don't worry about anything, but in everything,
through prayer and petition with thanksgiving,
let your requests be made known to God.
Philippians 4:6 HCSB

If you are like most women, it is simply a fact of life: from time to time, you worry. You worry about health, about finances, about safety, about relationships, about family, and about countless other challenges of life, some great and some small. Where is the best place to take your worries? Take them to God. Take your troubles to Him, and your fears, and your sorrows.

Barbara Johnson correctly observed, "Worry is the senseless process of cluttering up tomorrow's opportunities with leftover problems from today." So if you'd like to make the most out of this day (and every one hereafter), turn your worries over to a Power greater than yourself . . . and spend your valuable time and energy solving the problems you can fix . . . while trusting God to do the rest.

This life of faith, then, consists in just this—being a child in the Father's house. Let the ways of childish confidence and freedom from care, which so please you and win your heart when you observe your own little ones, teach you what you should be in your attitude toward God.

Hannah Whitall Smith

Today is mine. Tomorrow is none of my business. If I peer anxiously into the fog of the future, I will strain my spiritual eyes so that I will not see clearly what is required of me now.

Elisabeth Elliott

TODAY'S PRAYER

Dear Lord, wherever I find myself, let me celebrate more and worry less. When my faith begins to waver, help me to trust You more. Then, with praise on my lips and the love of Your Son in my heart, let me live courageously, faithfully, prayerfully, and thankfully this day and every day. Amen

WHO RULES?

Can you search out the deep things of God?
Can you find out the limits of the Almighty?
They are higher than heaven—what can you do?
Deeper than Sheol—what can you know?
Their measure is longer than the earth
And broader than the sea.

Job 11:7-9 NKJV

God is sovereign. He reigns over the entire universe and He reigns over your little corner of that universe. Your challenge is to recognize God's sovereignty, to live in accordance with His commandments, and to trust His promises. Sometimes, of course, these tasks are easier said than done.

Your Heavenly Father may not always reveal Himself as quickly (or as clearly) as you would like. But rest assured: God is in control, God is here, and God intends to use you in wonderful, unexpected ways. He desires to lead you along a path of His choosing. Your challenge is to watch, to listen, to learn . . . and to follow. Today.

There is something incredibly comforting about knowing that the Creator is in control of your life.

Lisa Whelchel

Our God is the sovereign Creator of the universe! He loves us as His own children and has provided every good thing we have; He is worthy of our praise every moment.

Shirley Dobson

Either we are adrift in chaos or we are individuals, created, loved, upheld and placed purposefully, exactly where we are. Can you believe that? Can you trust God for that?

Elisabeth Elliot

TODAY'S PRAYER

Dear Lord, You are the sovereign God of the universe. I will obey Your commandments, Father, and I will study Your Word. I will seek Your will for my life, and I will allow Your Son to reign over my heart every day. Amen

DAY 81

TRUST HIM WHEN TIMES ARE TOUGH

*I called to the Lord in my distress; I called to my
God. From His temple He heard my voice.*

2 Samuel 22:7 HCSB

The Bible promises this: tough times are temporary but God's love is not—God's love lasts forever. So what does that mean to you? Just this: From time to time, everybody faces tough times, and so will you. And when tough times arrive, God will always stand ready to protect you and heal you.

Psalm 147 promises, "He heals the brokenhearted" (v. 3, NIV), but Psalm 147 doesn't say that He heals them instantly. Usually, it takes time (and maybe even a little help from you) for God to fix things. So if you're facing tough times, face them with God by your side. If you find yourself in any kind of trouble, pray about it and ask God for help. And be patient. God will work things out, just as He has promised, but He will do it in His own way and in His own time.

Adversity is always unexpected and unwelcomed. It is an intruder and a thief, and yet in the hands of God, adversity becomes the means through which His supernatural power is demonstrated.

Charles Stanley

When God allows extraordinary trials for His people, He prepares extraordinary comforts for them.

Corrie ten Boom

TODAY'S PRAYER

Heavenly Father, You are my strength and my protector. When I am troubled, You comfort me. Let me turn to You, Lord, when I am weak. In times of adversity, let me trust Your plan and Your will for my life. Your love is infinite, as is Your wisdom. Whatever my circumstances, Lord, let me always give the praise, and the thanks, and the glory to You. Amen

MAKE THE MOST OF
WHATEVER COMES

A man's heart plans his way,
but the Lord determines his steps.
Proverbs 16:9 HCSB

Sometimes, we must accept life on its terms, not our own. Life has a way of unfolding, not as we will, but as it will. And sometimes, there is precious little we can do to change things.

When events transpire that are beyond our control, we have a choice: we can either learn the art of acceptance, or we can make ourselves miserable as we struggle to change the unchangeable.

We must entrust the things we cannot change to God. Once we have done so, we can prayerfully and faithfully tackle the important work that He has placed before us: doing something about the things we can change . . . and doing it sooner rather than later.

Two words will help you cope when you run low on hope: accept and trust.

Charles Swindoll

It is always possible to do the will of God. In every place and time it is within our power to acquiesce in the will of God.

Elisabeth Elliot

The one true way of dying to self is the way of patience, meekness, humility, and resignation to God.

Andrew Murray

TODAY'S PRAYER

Dear Lord, let me live in the present, not the past. Let me focus on my blessings, not my sorrows. Give me the wisdom to be thankful for the gifts that I do have, and not bitter about the things that I don't have. Let me accept what was, let me give thanks for what is, and let me have faith in what most surely will be: the promise of eternal life with You. Amen

THE POWER OF ENCOURAGEMENT

Patience and encouragement come from God.
And I pray that God will help you all agree with
each other the way Christ Jesus wants.

Romans 15:5 NCV

In his letter to the Ephesians, Paul writes, "Do not let any unwholesome talk come out of your mouths, but only what is helpful for building others up according to their needs, that it may benefit those who listen" (v. 29 NIV). This passage reminds us that we are instructed to choose our words carefully so as to build others up through wholesome, honest encouragement. How can we build others up? By celebrating their victories and their accomplishments.

Today, look for the good in others and celebrate the good that you find. When you do, you'll be a powerful force of encouragement in your corner of the world . . . and a worthy servant to your God.

Always stay connected to people and seek out things that bring you joy. Dream with abandon. Pray confidently.

Barbara Johnson

A single word, if spoken in a friendly spirit, may be sufficient to turn one from dangerous error.

Fanny Crosby

One of the ways God refills us after failure is through the blessing of Christian fellowship. Just experiencing the joy of simple activities shared with other children of God can have a healing effect on us.

Anne Graham Lotz

TODAY'S PRAYER

Dear Lord, let me celebrate the accomplishments of others. Make me a source of genuine, lasting encouragement to my family and friends. And let my words and deeds be worthy of Your Son, the One who gives me strength and salvation, this day and for all eternity. Amen

PUT FAITH ABOVE FEELINGS

Now the just shall live by faith.
Hebrews 10:38 NKJV

Who is in charge of your emotions? Is it you, or have you formed the unfortunate habit of letting other people—or troubling situations—determine the quality of your thoughts and the direction of your day? If you're wise—and if you'd like to build a better life for yourself and your loved ones—you'll learn to control your emotions before your emotions control you.

Sometime during this day, you will probably be gripped by a strong negative feeling. Distrust it. Reign it in. Test it. And turn it over to God. Your emotions will inevitably change; God will not. So trust Him completely as you watch those negative feelings slowly evaporate into thin air—which, of course, they will.

I may no longer depend on pleasant impulses to bring me before the Lord. I must rather respond to principles I know to be right, whether I feel them to be enjoyable or not.

Jim Elliot

Emotions we have not poured out in the safe hands of God can turn into feelings of hopelessness and depression. God is safe.

Beth Moore

Before you can dry another's tears, you too must weep.

Barbara Johnson

TODAY'S PRAYER

Father, You are my strength and my refuge. As I journey through this day, I will encounter events that cause me emotional distress. Lord, when I am troubled, let me turn to You. Keep me steady, Lord, and in those difficult moments, renew a right spirit inside my heart. Amen

RETURN GOD'S LOVE
BY SHARING IT

Dear friends, if God loved us in this way,
we also must love one another.
1 John 4:11 HCSB

Because God's power is limitless, it is far beyond the comprehension of mortal minds. But even though we cannot fully understand the heart of God, we can be open to God's love.

God's ability to love is not burdened by temporal boundaries or by earthly limitations. The love that flows from the heart of God is infinite—and today presents yet another opportunity to celebrate that love.

You are a glorious creation, a unique individual, a beautiful example of God's handiwork. God's love for you is limitless. Accept that love, acknowledge it, and be grateful.

There is no pit so deep that God's love is not deeper still.

Corrie ten Boom

Snuggle in God's arms. When you are hurting, when you feel lonely or left out, let Him cradle you, comfort you, reassure you of His all-sufficient power and love.

Kay Arthur

Being loved by Him whose opinion matters most gives us the security to risk loving, too—even loving ourselves.

Gloria Gaither

TODAY'S PRAYER

Dear God, You are love. You love me, Father, and I love You. As I love You more, Lord, I am also able to love my family and friends more. I will be Your loving servant, Heavenly Father, today and throughout eternity. Amen

CHOOSING TO STAND UP FOR YOUR BELIEFS

Souls who follow their hearts thrive;
fools bent on evil despise matters of soul.

Proverbs 13:19 MSG

We must do our best to make sure that our actions are accurate reflections of our beliefs. Our theology must be demonstrated, not only by our words but, more importantly, by our actions. In short, we should be practical women, quick to act upon the beliefs that we hold most dear.

We may proclaim our beliefs to our hearts' content, but our proclamations will mean nothing—to others or to ourselves—unless we accompany our words with deeds that match. The sermons that we live are far more compelling than the ones we preach.

Like it or not, your life is an accurate reflection of your creed. If this fact gives you cause for concern, don't bother talking about the changes that you intend to make—make them. Now.

Jesus taught that the evidence that confirms our leaps of faith comes after we risk believing, not before.

Gloria Gaither

Faith sees the invisible, believes the unbelievable, and receives the impossible.

Corrie ten Boom

Every man must do two things alone; he must do his own believing and his own dying.

Martin Luther

Understanding is the reward of faith. Therefore, seek not to understand that you may believe, but believe that you may understand.

St. Augustine

TODAY'S PRAYER

Heavenly Father, I believe in You, and I believe in Your Word. Help me to live in such a way that my actions validate my beliefs—and let the glory be Yours forever. Amen

KEEP PRAYING AND
KEEP GROWING

Like newborn infants, desire the unadulterated
spiritual milk, so that you may grow
by it in your salvation.
1 Peter 2:2 HCSB

When will you be a "fully-grown" Christian woman? Hopefully never—or at least not until you arrive in heaven! As a believer living here on planet earth, you're never "fully grown"; you always have the potential to keep growing.

Would you like a time-tested formula for spiritual growth? Here it is: keep studying God's Word, keep obeying His commandments, keep praying (and listening for answers), and keep trying to live in the center of God's will. When you do, you'll never stay stuck for long. You will, instead, be a growing Christian . . . and that's precisely the kind of Christian God wants you to be.

If you want to discover your spiritual gifts, start obeying God. As you serve Him, you will find that He has given you the gifts that are necessary to follow through in obedience.

Anne Graham Lotz

We set our eyes on the finish line, forgetting the past, and straining toward the mark of spiritual maturity and fruitfulness.

Vonette Bright

A spiritual gift is a manifestation of God at work through you. God works in and through you to bear fruit. The focus is on God and what He does through you.

Henry Blackaby and Claude King

TODAY'S PRAYER

Dear Lord, thank You for the opportunity to walk with Your Son. And, thank You for the opportunity to grow closer to You each day. I thank You for the person I am . . . and for the person I can become. Amen

EXPERIENCING SILENCE

Be still, and know that I am God.

Psalm 46:10 NKJV

The world seems to grow louder day by day, and our senses seem to be invaded at every turn. If we allow the distractions of a clamorous society to separate us from God's peace, we do ourselves a profound disservice. Our task, as dutiful believers, is to carve out moments of silence in a world filled with noise.

If we are to maintain righteous minds and compassionate hearts, we must take time each day for prayer and for meditation. We must make ourselves still in the presence of our Creator. We must quiet our minds and our hearts so that we might sense God's will and His love.

Has the busy pace of life robbed you of the peace that God has promised? Nothing is more important than the time you spend with God. So be still and claim the inner peace that is found in the silent moments you spend with God.

Let your loneliness be transformed into a holy aloneness. Sit still before the Lord. Remember Naomi's word to Ruth: "Sit still, my daughter, until you see how the matter will fall."

Elisabeth Elliot

Because Jesus Christ is our Great High Priest, not only can we approach God without a human "go-between," we can also hear and learn from God in some sacred moments without one.

Beth Moore

In the soul-searching of our lives, we are to stay quiet so we can hear Him say all that He wants to say to us in our hearts.

Charles Swindoll

TODAY'S PRAYER

Dear Lord, help me remember the importance of silence. Help me discover quiet moments throughout the day so that I can sense Your presence and Your love. Amen

GOD'S TIMETABLE

He has made everything appropriate in its time.
He has also put eternity in their hearts, but man
cannot discover the work God has done from
beginning to end.
Ecclesiastes 3:11 HCSB

I f you sincerely seek to be a woman of faith, then you must learn to trust God's timing. You will be sorely tempted, however, to do otherwise. Because you are a fallible human being, you are impatient for things to happen. But, God knows better.

God's plan does not always happen in the way that we would like or at the time of our own choosing. Our task—as believing Christians who trust in a benevolent, all-knowing Father—is to wait patiently for God to reveal Himself. And reveal Himself He will. Always. But until God's perfect plan is made known, we must walk in faith and never lose hope. And we must continue to trust Him. Always.

He whose attitude towards Christ is correct does indeed ask "in His Name" and receives what he asks for if it is something which does not stand in the way of his salvation. He gets it, however, only when he ought to receive it, for certain things are not refused us, but their granting is delayed to a fitting time.

St. Augustine

We must leave it to God to answer our prayers in His own wisest way. Sometimes, we are so impatient and think that God does not answer. God always answers! He never fails! Be still. Abide in Him.

Mrs. Charles E. Cowman

TODAY'S PRAYER

Dear Lord, Your timing is seldom my timing, but Your timing is always right for me. You are my Father, and You have a plan for my life that is grander than I can imagine. When I am impatient, remind me that You are never early or late . . . You are always on time. Amen

CHOOSING TO LET GOD TRANSFORM YOUR LIFE

Your old life is dead. Your new life, which is your real life—even though invisible to spectators— is with Christ in God. He is your life.

Colossians 3:3 MSG

Think, for a moment, about the "old" you, the person you were before you invited Christ to reign over your heart. Now, think about the "new" you, the person you have become since then. Is there a difference between the "old" you and the "new and improved" version? There should be! That difference should be noticeable not only to you but also to others.

The Bible clearly teaches that when we welcome Christ into our hearts, we become new creations through Him. Our challenge, of course, is to behave ourselves like new creations. When we do, God fills our hearts, He blesses our endeavors, and transforms our lives . . . forever.

If you are God's child, you are no longer bound to your past or to what you were. You are a brand new creature in Christ Jesus.

Kay Arthur

Conversion is not a blind leap into the darkness. It is a joyous leap into the light that is the love of God.

Corrie ten Boom

There is so much Heaven around us now if we have eyes for it, because eternity starts when we give ourselves to God.

Gloria Gaither

TODAY'S PRAYER

Lord, when I accepted Jesus as my personal Savior, You changed me forever and made me whole. Let me share Your Son's message with my friends, with my family, and with the world. You are a God of love, redemption, conversion, and salvation. I will praise You today and forever. Amen

DAY 91

BEYOND FEAR

Even when I go through the darkest valley,
I fear [no] danger, for You are with me.
Psalm 23:4 HCSB

A terrible storm rose quickly on the Sea of Galilee, and the disciples were afraid. Although they had witnessed many miracles, the disciples feared for their lives, so they turned to Jesus, and He calmed the waters and the wind.

The next time you find yourself facing a fear-provoking situation, remember that the One who calmed the wind and the waves is also your personal Savior. Then ask yourself which is stronger: your faith or your fear. The answer should be obvious. So, when the storm clouds form overhead and you find yourself being tossed on the stormy seas of life, remember this: Wherever you are, God is there, too. And, because He cares for you, you are protected.

Worry is a cycle of inefficient thoughts whirling around a center of fear.

Corrie ten Boom

God shields us from most of the things we fear, but when He chooses not to shield us, He unfailingly allots grace in the measure needed.

Elisabeth Elliot

Fear and doubt are conquered by a faith that rejoices. And faith can rejoice because the promises of God are as certain as God Himself.

Kay Arthur

TODAY'S PRAYER

Dear Lord, when I am fearful, keep me mindful that You are my protector and my salvation. Thank You, Father, for a perfect love that casts out fear. Because of You, I can live courageously and faithfully this day and every day. Amen

DAY 92

ESTABLISH A GROWING RELATIONSHIP WITH JESUS

But whoever keeps His word, truly in him
the love of God is perfected. This is how we know
we are in Him: the one who says he remains
in Him should walk just as He walked.
1 John 2:5-6 HCSB

Who's the best friend this world has ever had? Jesus, of course. And when you form a life-changing relationship with Him, He will be your best friend, too . . .

Jesus has offered to share the gifts of everlasting life and everlasting love with the world and with you. If you make mistakes, He'll stand by you. If you fall short of His commandments, He'll still love you. If you feel lonely or worried, He can touch your heart and lift your spirits.

Jesus wants you to enjoy a happy, healthy, abundant life. He wants you to walk with Him and to share His Good News. You can do it. And with a friend like Jesus, you will.

Tell me the story of Jesus. Write on my heart every word. Tell me the story most precious, sweetest that ever was heard.

Fanny Crosby

Jesus makes God visible. But that truth does not make Him somehow less than God. He is equally supreme with God.

Anne Graham Lotz

The crucial question for each of us is this: What do you think of Jesus, and do you yet have a personal acquaintance with Him?

Hannah Whitall Smith

TODAY'S PRAYER

Dear Lord, today I will abide in Jesus. I will look to Him as my Savior, and I will follow in His footsteps. Thank You, Lord, for Your Son. Today, I will count Him as my dearest friend, and I will share His transforming message with a world in desperate need of His peace. Amen

THE ULTIMATE CHOICE

*For God so loved the world that He gave
His only begotten Son, that whoever believes in Him
should not perish but have everlasting life.*

John 3:16 NKJV

Eternal life is not an event that begins when you die. Eternal life begins when you invite Jesus into your heart right here on earth. So it's important to remember that God's plans for you are not limited to the ups and downs of everyday life. If you've allowed Jesus to reign over your heart, you've already begun your eternal journey.

As mere mortals, our vision for the future, like our lives here on earth, is limited. God's vision is not burdened by such limitations: His plans extend throughout all eternity.

Let us praise God for His priceless gift, and let us share the Good News with all who cross our paths. We return our Father's love by accepting His grace and by sharing His message and His love.

God has promised us abundance, peace, and eternal life. These treasures are ours for the asking; all we must do is claim them. One of the great mysteries of life is why on earth do so many of us wait so very long to lay claim to God's gifts?

Marie T. Freeman

Like a shadow declining swiftly . . . away . . . like the dew of the morning gone with the heat of the day; like the wind in the treetops, like a wave of the sea, so are our lives on earth when seen in light of eternity.

Ruth Bell Graham

TODAY'S PRAYER

I know, Lord, that this world is not my home; I am only here for a brief while. And, You have given me the priceless gift of eternal life through Your Son Jesus. Keep the hope of heaven fresh in my heart, and, while I am in this world, help me to pass through it with faith in my heart and praise on my lips . . . for You. Amen

PRAY EARLY AND OFTEN

Rejoice always! Pray constantly.
Give thanks in everything,
for this is God's will for you in Christ Jesus.
1 Thessalonians 5:16-18 HCSB

As the old saying goes, if it's big enough to worry about, it's big enough to pray about. Yet sometimes, we don't pray about the specific details of our lives. Instead, we may offer general prayers that are decidedly heavy on platitudes and decidedly light on particulars.

The next time you pray, try this: be very specific about the things you ask God to do. Of course God already knows precisely what you need—He knows infinitely more about your life than you do—but you need the experience of talking to your Creator in honest, unambiguous language.

So today, don't be vague with God. Tell Him exactly what you need. He doesn't need to hear the details, but you do.

God says we don't need to be anxious about anything; we just need to pray about everything.

Stormie Omartian

What God gives in answer to our prayers will always be the thing we most urgently need, and it will always be sufficient.

Elisabeth Elliot

Your family and friends need your prayers and you need theirs. And God wants to hear those prayers. So what are you waiting for?

Marie T. Freeman

When the Holy Spirit comes to dwell within us, I believe we gain a built-in inclination to take our concerns and needs to the Lord in prayer.

Shirley Dobson

TODAY'S PRAYER

Dear Lord, I will be a woman of prayer. I will take everything to You in prayer, and when I do, I will trust Your answers. Amen

OBEDIENCE NOW

Not everyone who says to Me, "Lord, Lord!"
will enter the kingdom of heaven, but the one who
does the will of My Father in heaven.
Matthew 7:21 HCSB

God's laws are eternal and unchanging: obedience leads to abundance and joy; disobedience leads to disaster. God has given us a guidebook for righteous living called the Holy Bible. If we trust God's Word and live by it, we are blessed. But, if we choose to ignore God's commandments, the results are as predictable as they are tragic.

Do you seek God's peace and His blessings? Then obey Him. When you're faced with a difficult choice or a powerful temptation, seek God's counsel and trust the counsel He gives. Invite God into your heart and live according to His commandments. When you do, you will be blessed today, and tomorrow, and forever.

Let us never suppose that obedience is impossible or that holiness is meant only for a select few. Our Shepherd leads us in paths of righteousness—not for our name's sake but for His.

Elisabeth Elliot

The cross that Jesus commands you and me to carry is the cross of submissive obedience to the will of God, even when His will includes suffering and hardship and things we don't want to do.

Anne Graham Lotz

You may not always see immediate results, but all God wants is your obedience and faithfulness.

Vonette Bright

TODAY'S PRAYER

Dear Lord, make me a woman who is obedient to Your Word. Let me live according to Your commandments. Direct my path far from the temptations and distractions of this world. And, let me discover Your will and follow it, Lord, this day and always. Amen

DAY 96

FIND THE COURAGE TO FOLLOW GOD

Be strong and courageous, and do the work.
Don't be afraid or discouraged,
for the Lord God, my God, is with you.
He won't leave you or forsake you.
1 Chronicles 28:20 HCSB

Life can be difficult and discouraging at times. During our darkest moments, we can depend upon our friends and family, and upon God. When we do, we find the courage to face even the darkest days with hopeful hearts and willing hands.

So the next time you find your courage tested to the limit, remember that you're probably stronger than you think. And remember—with you, your friends, your family and your God all working together, you have nothing to fear.

Just as courage is faith in good, so discouragement is faith in evil, and, while courage opens the door to good, discouragement opens it to evil.

Hannah Whitall Smith

What is courage? It is the ability to be strong in trust, in conviction, in obedience. To be courageous is to step out in faith—to trust and obey, no matter what.

Kay Arthur

If a person fears God, he or she has no reason to fear anything else. On the other hand, if a person does not fear God, then fear becomes a way of life.

Beth Moore

TODAY'S PRAYER

Dear Lord, fill me with Your Spirit and help me face my challenges with courage and determination. Keep me mindful, Father, that You are with me always—and with You by my side, I have nothing to fear. Amen

SHARING YOUR FAITH

But sanctify the Lord God in your hearts,
and always be ready to give a defense to everyone
who asks you a reason for the hope that is in you.
1 Peter 3:15 HCSB

O ur personal testimonies are extremely important, but sometimes, because of shyness or insecurities, we're afraid to share our experiences. And that's unfortunate.

In his second letter to Timothy, Paul shares a message to believers of every generation when he writes, "God has not given us a spirit of timidity" (1:7). Paul's meaning is clear: When sharing our beliefs, we, as Christians, must be courageous, forthright, and unashamed.

We live in a world that desperately needs the healing message of Christ Jesus. Every believer, each in his or her own way, bears responsibility for sharing the Good News of our Savior. You know how He has touched your heart; help Him do the same for others.

There are many timid souls whom we jostle morning and evening as we pass them by; but if only the kind word were spoken they might become fully persuaded.

Fanny Crosby

Choose Jesus Christ! Deny yourself, take up the Cross, and follow Him—for the world must be shown. The world must see, in us, a discernible, visible, startling difference.

Elisabeth Elliot

TODAY'S PRAYER

Dear Lord, the life that I live and the words that I speak bear testimony to my faith. Make me a faithful servant of Your Son, and let my testimony be worthy of You. Let my words be sure and true, Lord, and let my actions point others to You. Amen

DAY 98

DON'T OVERESTIMATE THE IMPORTANCE OF APPEARANCES

Man does not see what the Lord sees, for man sees what is visible, but the Lord sees the heart.

1 Samuel 16:7 HCSB

Are you worried about keeping up appearances? As a result, do you spend too much time, energy, or money on things that are intended to make you look good? If so, you are certainly not alone. Our society focuses intently upon such appearances. We are told time and again that we can't be "too thin or too rich." But in truth, the important things in life have little to do with food, fashion, fame, or fortune.

Today, spend less time trying to please the world and more time trying to please your earthly family and your Father in heaven. Focus on pleasing your God and your loved ones, and don't worry too much about trying to impress the folks you happen to pass on the street.

Outside appearances, things like the clothes you wear or the car you drive, are important to other people but totally unimportant to God. Trust God.

Marie T. Freeman

It is comfortable to know that we are responsible to God and not to man. It is a small matter to be judged of man's judgement.

Lottie Moon

Fashion is an enduring testimony to the fact that we live quite consciously before the eyes of others.

John Eldredge

TODAY'S PRAYER

Dear Lord, the world sees only my outside appearance, but You see my heart. Today, I will focus, not on outward appearances, but on the reality of Your eternal love for me. Amen

DAY 99

LIVE ON PURPOSE

*I, therefore, the prisoner in the Lord, urge you to
walk worthy of the calling you have received.*

Ephesians 4:1 HCSB

"What on earth does God intend for
me to do with my life?" It's an easy
question to ask but, for many of
us, a difficult question to answer. Why? Because
God's purposes aren't always clear to us. Sometimes we wander aimlessly in a wilderness of our
own making. And sometimes, we struggle mightily against God in an unsuccessful attempt to find
success and happiness through our own means,
not His.

If you're a woman who sincerely seeks God's
guidance, He will give it. But, He will make His
revelations known to you in a way and in a time
of His choosing, not yours, so be patient. If you
prayerfully petition God and work diligently to
discern His intentions, He will, in time, lead you
to a place of joyful abundance and eternal peace.

Sometimes, God's intentions will be clear to you; other times, God's plan will seem uncertain at best. But even on those difficult days when you are unsure which way to turn, you must never lose sight of these overriding facts: God created you for a reason; He has important work for you to do; and He's waiting patiently for you to do it.

And the next step is up to you.

Yesterday is just experience but tomorrow is glistening with purpose—and today is the channel leading from one to the other.

Barbara Johnson

TODAY'S PRAYER

Dear Lord, I know that You have a purpose for my life, and I will seek that purpose today and every day that I live. Let my actions be pleasing to You, and let me share Your Good News with a world that so desperately needs Your healing hand and the salvation of Your Son. Amen

TACKLING TOUGH TIMES

God is our refuge and strength,
a very present help in trouble.

Psalm 46:1 NKJV

W omen of all generations have experienced adversity, and this generation is no different. But, today's women face challenges that previous generations could have scarcely imagined. Thankfully, although the world continues to change, God's love remains constant. He remains ready to comfort us and strengthen us whenever we turn to Him.

If you are like most women, it is simply a fact of life: from time to time, you worry. You worry about health, about finances, about safety, about relationships, about family, and about countless other challenges of life, some great and some small. Where is the best place to take your worries? Take them to God. Take your troubles to Him, and your fears, and your sorrows. Seek protection from the One who cannot be moved.

We all go through pain and sorrow, but the presence of God, like a warm, comforting blanket, can shield us and protect us, and allow the deep inner joy to surface, even in the most devastating circumstances.

Barbara Johnson

Recently I've been learning that life comes down to this: God is in everything. Regardless of what difficulties I am experiencing at the moment, or what things aren't as would like them to be, I look at the circumstances and say, "Lord, what are you trying to teach me?"

Catherine Marshall

TODAY'S PRAYER

Dear Lord, when I am troubled, You heal me. When I am afraid, You protect me. When I am discouraged, You lift me up. You are my unending source of strength, Lord. In times of adversity, let me trust Your plan and Your will for my life. And whatever my circumstances, Lord, let me always give the thanks and the glory to You. Amen

For I have given you an example that you also should do just as I have done for you.

John 13:15 HCSB